# Psychotherapy Supervision and Consultation in Clinical Practice

# Psychotherapy Supervision and Consultation in Clinical Practice

Edited by
Judith H. Gold

JASON ARONSON
*Lanham • Boulder • New York • Toronto • Oxford*

Published in the United States of America
by Jason Aronson
An imprint of Rowman & Littlefield Publishers, Inc.

A wholly owned subsidiary of
The Rowman & Littlefield Publishing Group, Inc.
4501 Forbes Boulevard, Suite 200, Lanham, Maryland 20706
www.rowmanlittlefield.com

PO Box 317
Oxford
OX2 9RU, UK



British Library Cataloguing in Publication Information Available

**Library of Congress Cataloging-in-Publication Data**

Psychotherapy supervision and consultation in clinical practice / edited by Judith H. Gold.
p. cm.
ISBN-13: 978-0-7657-0399-6 (cloth : alk. paper)
ISBN-10: 0-7657-0399-8 (cloth : alk. paper)
1. Psychotherapists—Supervision of. 2. Psychotherapy—Study and teaching. I. Gold, Judith H., 1941–

RC459.P76 2006
616.89'14—dc22 2005037366

Printed in the United States of America

∞™ The paper used in this publication meets the minimum requirements of American National Standard for Information Sciences—Permanence of Paper for Printed Library Materials, ANSI/NISO Z39.48-1992.

# Contents

# I

# INTRODUCTION

# Introduction

*Robert Michels*

Caring for psychiatric patients is difficult and challenging, and those who do so face complicated and unusual tasks.

First and foremost, they work with people who, by definition, are hard to understand and not always collaborative. They must employ a wide variety of methods—biologic, psychologic, and social. Although there is a growing body of empirical evidence concerning the effectiveness of these methods, the evidence rarely prescribes what a given therapist should do with a given patient at a given point in time. There are a seemingly infinite number of intervening variables: patient variables, such as comorbidities, life situations, life histories, and fantasies about illness and treatment; therapist variables, such as knowledge, experience, career trajectories, and theoretical and personal biases; and situational variables, such as the social and economic context of the treatment, its anticipated intensity, and the time frame. As a result, there is rarely a single right way to treat a patient, although there are often many wrong ways, and therapists do not learn "right ways" as much as learn how to proceed to plan and conduct the treatment in the face of ambiguity and uncertainty.

How do they learn this? Like the conduct of therapy itself, they do so in every possible way. A professional who plans to work with the mentally ill has a responsibility to know what is known and to learn what can be learned through didactic instruction, books, lectures, and journals. Case conferences are valuable, providing accounts of how others see problems and how they go about trying to solve them. Many who conduct psychotherapy find their own personal psychotherapy to be helpful. Learning about transference or resistance is like learning about swimming or dancing; there is a limit to what didactic instruction can achieve. One has to experience it directly in order to understand what it is about. When all goes well, these several methods, combined with clinical experience, lead to a therapist who is prepared to work with patients. Paradoxically, clinical experience can be valuable even if it is experience of failure. One can learn from mistakes if one is able to examine and reflect on them. In psychiatry, as in the rest of medicine, the usual principles of training have the novice work as an apprentice for a relatively long period of time so that the first time he is alone in a clinical situation, he has already had the experience of having done it many times in the past.

And then there is supervision, the subject of this book. Most experienced psychotherapists would agree with everything that I have said but would also agree that in spite of this, the most important component of their psychotherapeutic education has been supervision. Furthermore, as this book uniquely discusses, supervision is the experience that is likely to continue after formal training has been completed and to influence and shape professional development throughout the therapist's career.

Supervision involves talking about one's work with another. It occurs in every conceivable permutation and is as varied as psychotherapy itself. The other may be an individual or a group, a senior mentor, or a peer, someone who is simultaneously administering or evaluating one's work or is seen in a totally private and protected relationship. It may occur as a single event or a regular periodic meeting. It can focus on the patient, the therapist, or the therapeutic process and may shift among these domains. The goals of supervision also vary. It can provide quality assurance (including the maintenance of appropriate boundaries) for the patient, support and reassurance for the therapist, or an opportunity for professional learning and growth for the therapist (and, probably most often, a mix of these with the proportions shifting from time to time). It may include didactic teaching (defining a concept or suggesting a reading), but that should not be its central theme. It is usually differentiated from administration (supervision requires an atmosphere of tolerance and safety, with support for self-disclosure, while even the gentlest of administrative relationships may lead to some wariness on the part of the therapist). There has been particular concern to differentiate supervision from personal psychotherapy—supervision has a goal, a focus, and boundaries that are quite different from those of psychotherapy, and the skilled supervisor respects and maintains these in spite of temptations to blur them.

This book explores psychotherapy supervision from a variety of perspectives. We hear from both supervisors and supervisees, from early-career clinicians, and from senior members of the profession. The role of supervision in the therapist's professional development, particularly after formal training has been completed, is emphasized throughout. Difficult and special issues are faced, such as management of the patient's response to the particulars of the therapist, especially those that might be stigmatizing, or the supervision of boundary crossing and even of potential boundary violation.

The supervisory autobiographies of several supervisees trace their experiences as they complete their training and pursue their careers. Particularly interesting is the extension of supervision, which began as a tool in the teaching of psychodynamic psychotherapies to its use in other types of psychotherapy, case management, and clinical administration.

Supervision does not transform a poor therapist into a good one, but it can help any therapist become a better one. It is a method that is peculiarly suited to its subject matter—highly individual, a mixture of art and science, centered on an intense personal relationship, and based on a mixture of understanding and insight, emotional learning, and the transforming potential of human relationships. We are indebted to Dr. Gold and her colleagues for providing views of what happens in a variety of types of supervision and enhancing our understanding of the difference it can make and how it does so.

# 1

# Why Psychotherapy Supervision Is Essential for Mental Health Professionals

*Judith H. Gold*

Susan Smith is a staff psychiatrist in a busy urban general hospital. She has held this position since passing her examinations three years ago. The psychiatry department is understaffed, and she has been placed in a senior position overseeing an acute care ward where she is the psychiatrist in charge and is also responsible for teaching residents and other mental health staff. Susan works long hours and also has family responsibilities. Lately, she is frequently angry with some of her patients and worrying about others. She feels tired and overwhelmed by her responsibilities. A colleague suggests that Susan seek supervision immediately.

John Smith is a caseworker in a government family services department. Trained as a social worker, he now has between eighty and one hundred active files and tries to oversee the welfare of all the involved children. Conscious also of recent legal action regarding the responsibility of care by social workers for these children, he feels increasingly pressured to follow all his cases closely. He often fears for his safety, having been threatened by angry parents and visiting families on his own because of a lack of staffing. In addition, he provides psychotherapy for many of the children placed in foster care and for some of the parents. Recently, one parent died by suicide after John had removed his children from his care. John is considering resigning and finding another career.

Jane Smith is an occupational therapist working in a community mental health clinic. With a policy of team care for patients, she finds herself providing long-term psychotherapy or case management for patients with a variety of mental health disorders. Often she feels that her cases are complex and tax her expertise. She frequently asks the psychiatrists who provide psychopharmacological management and oversight for advice but feels increasingly overwhelmed.

These are a few examples of people working in an increasingly complex and demanding mental health system. Understaffed usually, frustrated by demands placed on them, and conscientiously trying to service their clientele, mental health professionals often feel inadequately trained to manage the psychological health of their patients. Whether in private practice or in public service, many face an underfunded and understaffed system with growing scrutiny of their professional behavior. In other settings, clinicians are asked to treat patients in collaboration with another mental health professional and must then find ways, together with the other clinician, to work optimally with the patient, frequently without adequate training in the complexities of split treatment. Further, with the cutbacks in funding for long-term psychotherapies by many insurers, many clinicians find themselves in conflict between their recognition of the treatment best for the patient and the treatment that is fundable. In some areas, and in some countries, the shortage of trained mental health clinicians leads to pressure on the clinician to treat more patients more quickly, to work long hours, and to accept responsibilities beyond their training or experience.

While demands for evidence-based treatment protocols are growing, clinically it is known that all interactions between clinicians and patients have an interpersonal psychotherapeutic basis. Research has demonstrated that successful treatment requires a therapeutic alliance and that compliance with treatments is enhanced by such an alliance.[1, 2] Even very brief encounters engender some type of interpersonal reaction for both patient and clinician. Understanding and managing these interactions is an essential skill for every mental health professional and clinical team. When the factors influencing these interpersonal relationships are not appreciated or are overlooked, ignored, or mismanaged, treatment failures can ensue, as can boundary violations.

Requesting consultation with a senior colleague in specific incidents or arranging supervision on an ongoing basis can assist clinicians in all settings and circumstances. This book seeks to demonstrate the usefulness of consultation and supervision as well as to discuss the barriers perceived to exist in making such requests for assistance in increasing competency. We describe how both clinician and patient benefit. The idea for the book arose from reflection about the role of psychotherapy supervision in the work life of busy mental health professionals. This was precipitated by a discussion with some of the authors of the following chapters about the dissipation of a tradition of supervision and consultation among clinicians as therapeutic interventions centered more and more on psychopharmacology and case management rather than on psychodynamics and interpersonal interactions.

Books and papers on supervision tend to focus on trainees or on psychoanalytic case supervision. Little attention seems to have been paid to the need for psychotherapy supervision—or for consultation—for those clinicians in practice in the community. Clinical oversight and consultation is often available in hospital settings to assist in case management but appears to be rarely available for psychodynamic interactions and treatments. An extensive literature search conducted through Medline revealed few publications in the past two decades. Nevertheless, many professional organizations recommend ongoing supervision and consultation to their members. Emphasis on the importance of such activities is found in discussions of the avoidance of boundary violations and in practice guidelines such as the American Psychiatric Association's "Practice Guideline for the Treatment of Patients with Borderline Personality Disorder."[3, 4, 5]

Expertise as a psychotherapist continues to develop throughout one's career and does not culminate with graduation from a training program. Just as clinicians must constantly update their knowledge of psychopharmacology, the practice of any of the psychotherapies requires continuing attention to new theories, to new research data, and to the maintenance and improvement of therapeutic skills. While some of this can be acquired through reading and didactic courses, clinical interaction with others well versed in psychodynamic techniques and familiar with current theories and research is as useful for practitioners as for trainees.[6]

Furthermore, many mental health professionals, including psychiatrists, will find that their training has not prepared them for the complexities of practice. Courses during training provide a practical knowledge of psychotherapy sufficient to meet training and examination requirements. Many discover that this experience is insufficient and that they will benefit from learning more advanced techniques; some find that other skills are needed, especially when dealing with complex patients such as those with personality disorders. While professional associations are beginning to require competency in a number of psychotherapies, it is not uncommon for a professional working in a mental health clinic or practice to have expertise in only one modality, such as cognitive-behavioral therapy, interpersonal therapy, or dialectical behavior therapy. The difficult patient, the person with intractable depression, the poorly compliant person, and the person with complex psychosocial problems will strain the skills of these clinicians. In addition, many treatment settings will demand a broad range of psychotherapeutic skills from each clinician, especially in these times of restricted budgets and understaffing. A mental health professional in practice in a small or underserviced area may also discover that his or her training is inadequate to meet the therapeutic needs of clients. Additionally, some patients may arouse feelings in the clinician that can lead to a variety of boundary violations, from inappropriate treatment settings to overt sexual activity.

In all these instances, the clinician will benefit from supervision with their cases or, at least, from consultation with someone more expert. Finally, understanding the psychological functioning of an individual will assist in the development of a therapeutic alliance. The chapters that follow in this book discuss and illustrate all these points in detail.

Mental health professionals should be encouraged to seek supervision both to increase their understanding of underlying psychodynamics and to broaden their psychotherapeutic skills.[7] Organizations that maintain professional standards could offer credits for continuing education and maintenance of competency to both supervisee and supervisor, much as some now credit peer study groups.

Professionals with expertise in psychodynamic psychotherapy will also benefit from supervision to help maintain and extend their skills. Supervision also provides a forum for addressing ethical concerns and boundary issues as well as transference and countertransference. It can also help those who work in multidisciplinary teams develop an understanding of complex team dynamics that may be affecting patients' treatment. Supervision can also assist the professional in becoming aware of the underlying dynamics in patients who have seemingly intractable symptoms or who are noncompliant. When the clinician is experiencing personal difficulties, supervision can be essential for effective clinical practice.[8]

## THE SUPERVISORY PROCESS

The role of the supervisor is multifaceted but does not include providing treatment for that person. If the supervisee would benefit from psychiatric or psychological treatment, that must be obtained elsewhere. The supervisor is also not a cotherapist and does not actively participate in the treatment of the patient/client under discussion during the supervision. The supervisor must also be aware of his or her motivation in agreeing to supervise and be sensitive to the supervisee's level of self-esteem as well as transference issues.[9] A discussion of training for supervisors can be found in chapter 5.

Psychotherapy supervision of both trainees and clinicians demands the sensitivity of a good teacher and the intuitive skills of a psychotherapist. Supervisees should feel accepted and respected while being assisted to develop their therapeutic expertise. In all instances, the process involves confidentiality, both for the supervisee and for content related to the patient(s). The supervisor does not permit boundary violations to occur between them.

This also provides a modeling of interpersonal professional behavior for the supervisee.

Supervision sessions may center on one patient's therapy or may vary from session to session, depending on the clinician's perceived need for assistance. The focus may be on appreciating psychodynamics, aspects of psychotherapeutic technique, and the interaction between patient and therapist. The relationship between the supervisor and supervisee is not the main focus but is discussed in terms of the interaction between the two of them about the supervisory content. The purpose of the supervision is learning, not personal development.

In some instances, the supervisor is chosen as an expert on a particular type of psychotherapy or because of experience working with a certain diagnostic group. At other times, someone may be chosen because he or she is well versed in the management of the therapeutic alliance and transference/countertransference issues. In small communities, a clinician may request supervision from a respected colleague. The supervisee is encouraged to develop an empathic, psychodynamically educated view of the patient while also being introspective and self-aware. Technique is discussed, and interventions are suggested. The supervisor must be flexible and consider the supervisee's knowledge, experience, and insight. In other words, supervision must be conducted with awareness of the individual being supervised, much as psychotherapy treatment must be tailored to each individual client.

The supervisor must ascertain the level of knowledge of each supervisee since the supervision of someone with a limited background in psychotherapy and psychodynamics can be very difficult for both the supervisee and the supervisor. The goal of supervision, like that of therapy, is to have practitioners develop an internal supervisor—to learn how to watch themselves as well as the patient. During the process of supervision, the supervisor learns as well, reflecting on interactions with clients, improving skills, and learning new techniques. In fact, it is important to remain a student in that sense forever, or therapy will become ineffective as skills stagnate. In helping a supervisee develop a capacity to reflect on therapy as it proceeds, the supervisor encourages exploration and enquiry.[10] It has been said that the psychoanalytic supervisory process mirrors or parallels what is happening during the therapy.[11] However, much depends on the type of supervision being offered as well as on the type of psychotherapy. Brief psychodynamic psychotherapy and the interactive, interpersonal psychotherapies focus more on the therapeutic alliance than on transference/countertransference issues. Supervision of such cases follows the same model.

However, an element of transference and countertransference exists in all supervisory relationships. The supervisor will initially be cast into a role created by the supervisee's perceptions of the supervisor's reputation and personal qualities. Supervision, like psychotherapy and indeed any treatment, is an interaction between two people with individual personalities and experiences. While the literature on psychoanalysis seems to accept as a given that the supervisee may feel toward the supervisor as the patient does toward the supervisee, this does not occur routinely in the other psychotherapies. Nevertheless, the supervisor should remember and watch for this possibility.

The supervisor's role is that of a teacher or, at times, a consultant, and it should be remembered that every student learns differently. The supervisor's task is to assist the supervisee-clinician in observing both the patient and him- or herself and recognizing emotional reactions and defenses in each of them. This is one of the essential skills of a therapist: being able to interact with the patient while simultaneously observing the interaction and reflecting on and reacting to such observations. This must be taught to those new to psychotherapy through gentle questioning that allows them to tell the supervisor of what they are aware at each session. As Coburn states, supervision differs from therapy by "a mutual, reciprocal verbal exploration of both parties' countertransference experiences in relation to the patient at hand . . . a facet of this exploration should attend to the supervisor's ongoing invitation to the supervisee to reflect upon how the supervision experience is impacting the supervisee from a cognitive, affective, theoretical, and/or practical standpoint. This facet, if left unattended, can alter the manner in which the supervisee presents . . . clinical material" (488).[11]

Supervisees may not include all the information they have in their reports to the supervisor. The relationship with the supervisor, therefore, is important in facilitating as full disclosure as possible. A discussion of the impact of supervision on the supervisee should form a constant part of the process. Otherwise, as Coburn points out and as all those who have been involved with supervision know, two therapies may be occurring: the one actually taking place between clinician and patient and the one being discussed in supervision.

In discussing the supervision of students, Chagoya and Chagoya present a list of the usual supervisory activities that is also applicable to clinician-supervisees:

1. Focusing the student's attention on the blind spots of his or her understanding of the patient (transference and dynamics);
2. Pointing out the interventions (or the silences) determined by the student's countertransference as well as the effects of the student's behavior on the patient;
3. Providing for the student clinical examples of successful or failed interventions taken from the supervisor's practice; and
4. Commenting, when necessary, on the type of relationship the student establishes with the supervisor. (194)[12]

These authors recommend that a supervisor use suggestion, questioning, and examples to help the supervisee appreciate that awareness of the patient's "distress and overall mental state" is important, that an attitude of learning and listening for conscious and unconscious meaning is essential, and that there is "often no one correct response in a given clinical situation."[12]

The way in which a clinician utilizes the supervision will depend on his or her characteristic way of reacting to any teaching and also on the relationship with the supervisor. This is where it can become difficult to separate therapy and supervision. The supervisor may need to point out a supervisee's characteristic patterns and, if necessary, recommend personal therapy with someone else while helping the clinician recognize how these behaviors affect therapy with the patient as well as the supervision. In these situations, the supervisor may sometimes need to ask another supervisor for assistance with the supervision.

Supervision should begin with the understanding that any ethical violations will be reported to the relevant licensing authority, much as the clinician is bound to report criminal or threatening statements by a patient to the police. During the supervision sessions, the supervisor must remain alert to any possibility of boundary violations within the therapeutic relationship being supervised and address this with the supervisee immediately. As mentioned earlier, some clinicians will seek supervision because of their fear of impending boundary violations and their need for assistance in managing their feelings and behaviors. When the clinician-supervisee is involved in some interaction with the client that could lead to ethics procedures, professional board inquiries, or sanctions, the supervisor may feel an ethical dilemma between confidentiality and trust that the supervisee expects and his or her duty to report. In such instances, the supervisor is, in my view, bound by the duty to report. Supervisory aspects of boundary violations are discussed in detail in chapter 6.

## SUPERVISORY STYLES

Shanfield and Gil describe four types of supervisory style, paraphrased here, that are useful in describing the supervision of practicing clinicians as well as trainee psychiatrists:[13]

1. *The facilitator.* The style here is consultative. The supervisee brings concerns to the supervisor, including countertransference issues. It is an interactive type of supervision with both supervisor and supervisee determining the agenda of the supervisory session while the supervisor encourages a greater understanding of the psychotherapy process.
2. *The confrontative and directive.* Here interpretation is given by the supervisor who is in charge of the session. Both the patient's and the supervisee's issues are discussed.

3. *The expert.* In control of the supervision, the expert makes the patient the focus. Countertransference does not form part of the discussion.
4. *Task oriented.* Here the supervisor determines the work to be done in a session, focusing on content. Countertransference in either the therapy or the supervision is ignored (227–29).

The supervision of practicing clinicians has an additional feature in that it tends to be less formal than supervision of trainees. While the supervisor is still seen as such, here the supervision is collegial and has a peer-review aspect, including the absence of grades and assessments. Depending on the expertise of the supervisee, this supervision is more likely to be consultative in style.

Inexperienced clinicians usually require a more directive approach until they become more comfortable and reflective. The supervisor should be available for consultation in case an acute situation arises and the supervisee feels the need for consultation. The supervisor should attempt to convey the pleasure a therapist derives from the process of therapy as the patient learns and grows. Demonstrating that one enjoys one's work and is constantly learning from it is an important message.

As discussed previously, the style of supervision has an impact on the supervisee. The supervisor determines the supervisory approach with each supervisee and with each case presented. Sometimes the needs of the patient will prompt a more "expert" and directive supervision; in other instances, some supervisors may be so "reflective" as to be completely nondirective. Above all, a supervisor teaches effective psychotherapeutic techniques by helping the supervisee learn what works best for that clinician and each patient.

## VULNERABILITY OF THE SUPERVISEE

The style of supervision and the manner of the supervisor not only determine the type of supervisory process but also the relationship between supervisor and supervisee. Much like a therapeutic alliance, this has been called a learning, supervisory, or training alliance.[14] The quality of this alliance will affect the supervisee's ability and willingness to reflect back all that is known about the patient and the therapeutic exchange, including his or her countertransference. Anxiety in reporting to a supervisor centers on fear of having made an error, fear of being shamed, and a sense of being inadequate. The supervisor must often be teacher, consultant, and supportive counselor in turn to each supervisee. Each supervisor learns to carry out these roles within the parameters of his or her personality and theoretical beliefs about therapy.

Like all teachers, the supervisor should not be an inactive recipient of the supervisee's reporting. Rather, the role of supervisor is to receive a picture of what is happening between psychiatrist and patient and then help the supervisee develop an understanding of that interaction with the patient and what techniques are useful. An open exchange should take place between supervisor and supervisee in which they discuss their feelings about the patient and about the supervisory content and process.

Nigam et al. described the vulnerability felt by supervisees.[15] They reviewed the literature on supervision of students and identified factors involved in feelings of shame supervisees may have. These include problematic choice of patient, fear of being perceived as incompetent or inadequate, narcissistic injury, a demeaning and unsupportive supervisory style, and, as referred to previously, the supervisee's perception of the relationship between supervisor and supervisee. Personal revelation is often as difficult for therapists at the outset of supervision as for patients at the outset of therapy. It is the role of the supervisor to facilitate and encourage the supervisee's ability to be self-reflective and questioning as well as to develop psychotherapeutic skills.

The available literature often discusses difficulties associated with supervision, and, as noted, several studies of the perceptions of the supervisory process have been conducted. All these studies emphasize the importance of supervision for learning, training, and mentoring as well as role modeling. These studies also refer to feelings of incompetence and inadequacy, confusion between psychodynamic schools or theories, and the fear of shame in supervision.[15, 16] Professional pride—that is, giving up the expert professional role to be a student with another professional who is often perceived to be an expert therapist—may also add to the supervisee's reluctance to self-disclose. However, supervisees who have difficulties telling supervisors what occurred during a session and how they felt about it can learn from this to appreciate how difficult it is for a patient to speak openly. Revealing oneself to another demands trust in the other and allowing oneself to be vulnerable to the reactions and opinions of that person. For some clinicians, this return to the student role is threatening. In others, the supervisor is felt to be more than a teacher or mentor and is viewed in a parental, authoritative role. The supervisee in this transferential situation may become dependent on the supervisory sessions. It is incumbent on the supervisor to be aware of the possibility of these reactions and to respond with discussion if they occur.

In all instances, the content of the supervision remains confidential and private. For some clinicians, being supervised is also a fact that they prefer to remain confidential, and they react in a manner similar to that of patients when meeting the supervisor socially. Encountering other mental health professionals at the site of the supervision may also create discomfort. Here feelings of shame and inadequacy remain to be addressed during the supervision, and the supervisor must always be alert to this aspect of supervision. Group supervision, as discussed in the next chapter, is often practical when supervisors are scarce and is a venue in which such feelings may potentially arise. Supervisees may feel that they are exposing their psychotherapeutic abilities before peers as well as the supervisor. On the other hand, peer support and insights can be encouraging, as in any group process. The supervisor's attitude will determine the success or failure of the supervision, whether individual or group. As Rubin points out, the supervisor uses skills gained as a psychotherapist in conducting supervision: "identifying difficulties; considering the appropriate timing and focus of an intervention; having the ability to tolerate and contain the anxieties encountered on both sides; and finding the means to communicate with each other" (395).[17]

## SUPERVISION VERSUS THERAPY

What constitutes supervision, and what becomes therapy? Anything that impinges on the work with the patient is part of supervision, but the personal life and problems of the supervisee are not. Sometimes the dividing line is unclear. Characteristic personality traits that adversely affect the therapy can be pointed out and the need for psychotherapy elsewhere suggested. Countertransference reactions are part of the discussions in supervision; when such reactions indicate psychopathology and continually interfere with treatment, psychotherapy for the supervisee is to be recommended. The supervisor does not inquire about the conduct of that psychotherapy or participate in it.

## THEORETICAL ORIENTATION

The supervisor may be an adherent of one particular school of psychodynamic theory or practice. However, the supervisee should be encouraged to learn about several different approaches to the same case. The supervisor should assist the supervisee in developing a personally appropriate style of therapy and adherence to a particular psychodynamic perspective. That is to say not that every supervisor must possess knowledge and expertise in all aspects of psychotherapy but rather that each supervisor should assist and encourage supervisees to develop their own skills. The supervisor may suggest an approach in a particular aspect of the case being supervised, may give an example of what he or she would do in such a case, and then discuss this with the supervisee, who can adapt the technique. Much as in psychotherapy treatment, the clinician at first models his or her therapy through the interaction with the supervisor. The supervisor's "voice" may be a presence in the treatment sessions until the supervisee develops a personal style and therapeutic approach. As the supervisee's knowledge and skills grow, emphasis on technique becomes more generalized, and discussion of theory can increase. The supervisor becomes less directive and more consultative as the supervisee develops an internal supervisor.

Again, it must be emphasized that the potential for boundary violations exists within supervision much as it does within therapy. The supervisor's constant monitoring of his or her countertransference to the supervisee will serve to prevent such transgressions while offering another behavior modeling experience to the supervisee. When possible, participation in a supervisors' peer group can be invaluable. If not possible locally, the supervisor can consult by telephone with other supervisors from time to time.

## SUPERVISION OF EXPERIENCED PSYCHODYNAMIC THERAPISTS

Supervision of clinicians who already have psychodynamic skills demands a more consultative approach. Here the supervisor assists the clinician in dealing with a troubling aspect of a specific treatment, including transference and countertransference. The focus is on technique and on the therapist's feelings and thoughts about the patient and the process of therapy. Again, the supervisor might also make suggestions, offer examples from his or her own practice, and encourage the professional toward an understanding of the dynamics of the client and of the treatment process. In such instances, the supervisor is seen as a consultant rather than as a teacher offering regular supervisory sessions.

## BARRIERS TO SEEKING PSYCHOTHERAPY SUPERVISION OR CONSULTATION

Psychotherapy supervision is required during some professional training programs as part of the learning process. This supervision is often limited to the psychotherapy cases that are required for the satisfactory completion of training in some of the health professions. Although other interactions with patients may be influenced by clinical supervision, the trainee often proceeds on a daily basis with little oversight. Recent changes in training requirements for psychiatrists in the United States, for example, include the necessity for competency in five psychotherapies, including psychodynamic psychotherapy. While daily interpersonal interactions with patients, both in inpatient and outpatient settings, usually proceed without supervision, psychiatry residents in the United States are now required to have two hours of supervision each week during their training. However, many psychiatrists and other mental health clinicians in practice today will not have had the benefit of these educational advances.[6] Therefore, it is not surprising that, once in clinical practice, many commonly do not obtain supervision or consultation.

In addition, there are a number of barriers, both to becoming a supervisor and to seeking supervision. Those who do offer supervision do so on the basis of their own clinical experience, usually at the request of others who perceive these clinicians as having expertise in psychodynamic psychotherapy. Many feel unprepared to offer supervision and doubt their ability to supervise. Training as a mental health professional does not prepare one to be a supervisor any more than it trains one to be a teacher. Nevertheless, long experience treating patients helps develop psychotherapeutic skills that can be passed on to others through the supervisory process. A discussion of training to be a supervisor can be found in chapter 5.

As mentioned earlier, the shame that some feel when asking for supervision or consultation can be a barrier to proceeding. Seeking supervision is seen by some as an admission of inadequacy rather than as recognition of the need for consultation in difficult clinical situations or in developing psychotherapeutic techniques, thus improving patient care. We expect individuals with symptoms to seek treatment. However, many mental health professionals find it difficult to admit that they themselves might benefit from and ask for assistance with their practice. In contrast, consultation and supervision in psychopharmacological management is frequently requested.

This reluctance to obtain assistance with psychotherapeutic practice reflects not only fear of potential exposure as a poor clinician and therapist but also the paucity of psychotherapy training in many programs. Such training, when available at all, should involve more than obligatory seminars and case conferences; rather, it should involve learning by observing and listening to teachers who, as mental health professionals, approach every interaction with every client from a psychodynamic as well as a psychophysiological perspective. Training in psychotherapy should be broader than learning basic skills in cognitive-behavioral therapy. In psychiatry, for example, a number of educators have been emphasizing this approach in recent years. However, many academic psychiatrists who trained during the past several decades of focus on biological psychiatry are themselves not comfortable with the concepts that underlie the psychodynamic psychotherapies.[18, 19]

Furthermore, many programs are affected by the demands of managed care environments, and this may limit training that fosters an appreciation of the dynamics underlying every interaction with a patient. In addition, third-party reimbursement systems frequently have powerful financial disincentives to the provision of psychotherapy by psychiatrists, especially the psychodynamic psychotherapies.[20] Other mental health professionals often complete training having had no instruction in any psychotherapy or in psychodynamic theories yet are expected to provide psychotherapeutic care once working in the community. I discuss this point further in the next chapter.

Choosing a supervisor can also be problematic when an experienced clinician seeks supervision/consultation only from someone who has a similar theoretical and practical approach. Such a limitation may make obtaining supervision impossible in locations where there are few other clinicians. Finally, in some instances, the cost of supervision is seen as a barrier. The mental health professional may find it difficult or be unwilling to pay the fee charged by supervisors, much as do some clients. This may not be due to ambivalence over the need for supervision but at times is based purely on financial reality. Some supervisors are willing to structure a fee schedule in such circumstances.[21]

Many professionals practice in settings that provide little or no opportunity for interchange with colleagues in their discipline. The opportunity to discuss cases and the psychotherapeutic treatment of patients is often limited outside group and academic practices. And even in such practice situations, an exchange or consultation may not occur, especially if colleagues do not appear to share an interest in psychodynamics or even in the complexities of their interactions with their clients. This isolation hinders the development of skills and can lead to inadequate treatment and inappropriate behaviors. A discussion of ethical violations is the focus of chapter 6.

## NOTES

The terms "patient" and "client" are used interchangeably in this book and reflect the clinical focus of the authors. Portions of this chapter were published in J. H. Gold, "Reflections on Psychodynamic Psychotherapy Supervision for Psychiatrists in Clinical Practice," *Journal of Psychiatric Practice* 10, no. 3 (2004): 162–69.

1. William P. Henry et al., "Psychodynamic Approaches," in *Handbook of Psychotherapy and Behavioral Change*, 4th ed., ed. Allen E. Bergin and Sol L. Garfield (New York: Wiley, 1994), 467–508.
2. Frank R. Margison, "Measurement and Psychotherapy," *British Journal of Psychiatry* 17 (2000): 123–30.
3. Glen O. Gabbard and Sallye M. Wilkinson, *Management of Countertransference with Borderline Patients* (Washington, D.C.: American Psychiatric Press, 1994).
4. Stanley E. Greben and Ronald Ruskin, *Clinical Perspectives on Psychotherapy Supervision* (Washington, D.C.: American Psychiatric Press, 1994).
5. American Psychiatric Association, "Practice Guideline for the Treatment of Patients with Borderline Personality Disorder," *American Journal of Psychiatry* 158, suppl. 10 (2001): 158.

6. Carol A. Falender et al., "Defining Competencies in Psychology Supervision: A Consensus Statement," *Journal of Clinical Psychology* 60 (2004): 771–85.

7. Michelle Cleary and Adele Freeman, "The Cultural Realities of Clinical Supervision in an Acute Inpatient Mental Health Setting," *Issues in Mental Health Nursing* 26 (2005): 489–505.

8. Judith H. Gold and John C. Nemiah, eds., *Beyond Transference: When the Therapist's Real Life Intrudes* (Washington, D.C.: American Psychiatric Press, 1993).

9. Ety Berant et al., "Supervising Personality Assessment: The Integration of Intersubjective and Psychodynamic Elements in the Supervision Process," *Journal of Personality Assessment* 84 (2005): 205–12.

10. Sarah M. Whitman and E. Gardner Jacobs, "Responsibilities of the Psychotherapy Supervisor," *American Journal of Psychotherapy* 52 (1998): 166–75.

11. William J. Coburn, "The Vision in Supervision: Transference-Countertransference Dynamics and Disclosure in the Supervision Relationship," *Bulletin of the Menninger Clinic* 61 (1997): 481–94.

12. Leopoldo Chagoya and Charlotte Chagoya, "The Development of a Psychotherapy Supervisor," in *Clinical Perspectives on Psychotherapy Supervision*, ed. S. E. Greben and R. Ruskin (Washington, D.C.: American Psychiatric Press, 1994), 189–209.

13. Stephen B. Shanfield and Dorion Gil, "Styles of Psychotherapy Supervision," *Journal of Psychiatric Education* 9 (1985): 225–32.

14. Stephen A. Green, ed., *Limit Setting in Clinical Practice* (Washington, D.C.: American Psychiatric Press, 1988), 111.

15. Tara Nigam et al., "Impasses in the Supervisory Process: A Resident's Perspective," *American Journal of Psychotherapy* 51 (1997): 252–67.

16. Shmuel Fennig et al., "The Psychiatrist as Psychotherapist: The Problem of Identity," *American Journal of Psychotherapy* 47 (1993): 33–37.

17. Simon S. Rubin, "At the Border of Supervision: Critical Moments in Psychotherapists' Development," *American Journal of Psychotherapy* 43 (1989): 387–97.

18. Jerald Kay, "Integrated Treatment: An Overview," in *Integrated Treatment for Psychiatric Disorders*, vol. 20, ed. Jerald Kay (Washington, D.C.: American Psychiatric Publishing, 2001), 1.

19. Alan Tasman, "Teaching Psychodynamic Psychiatry during Medical School and Residency: Specific Skills and Beyond," *Journal of Psychotherapy Practice and Research* 8 (1999): 187–90.

20. Joyce C. West et al., "Economic Grand Rounds: Financial Disincentives for the Provision of Psychotherapy," *Psychiatric Services* 54 (2003): 1582–88.

21. Michael Townend, "Interprofessional Supervision from the Perspectives of Both Mental Health Nurses and Other Professionals in the Field of Cognitive Behavioral Psychotherapy," *Journal of Psychiatric Mental Health Nursing* 12 (2005): 582–88.

# 2

# Supervision: Models, Tools, and Supervisory Experiences

*Judith H. Gold*

A discussion of factors related to the need for supervision and obtaining supervision or consultation is contained in the first chapter. Such supervision can be individual or in a group. Furthermore, group supervision can take place with a few or many individuals. The principles of supervision as described in chapter 1 do not differ with the format. However, several factors can be more prominent and must be borne in mind by the supervisor when supervision is offered to a group rather than to an individual. These include the supervisee's reluctance to expose therapeutic skills and techniques to colleagues, as well as to the supervisor, with feelings of shame and inadequacy predominating; fear of criticism from colleagues; lack of trust in colleagues as well as in the supervisor; and concerns about confidentiality.

The workplace demands of busy mental health professionals usually limit the frequency of supervision. Unlike training programs where supervision is scheduled or required to occur weekly, in practice situations the clinician has to arrange for supervision voluntarily. This will have to take place, most often, outside the workplace. Time and financial considerations limit the frequency of the sessions. Occasionally, a crisis situation will result in the need for weekly supervision to be requested until the matter is resolved. Some clinicians then retreat from continuing supervision until the next crisis. Others make regularly scheduled supervision a part of a professional continuing education program. Much as when working with patients, the supervisor can only point out his or her perception of the supervisee's need for supervision or consultation but cannot compel participation.

At times, often because of a lack of resources, simultaneous supervision may be requested for a number of clinicians. This can take the form of a case presentation, which is then the basis for the supervisory session, with a different participant in the supervisee role at each session. In other instances, the supervisor is presented with a generalized clinical problem, such as patients who self-harm, and asked to discuss therapeutic solutions and approaches with the supervisees. In this chapter, I discuss these supervisory experiences, illustrated with comments from supervisees.

## CASE PRESENTATION MODEL

This method is very useful when supervisory resources are limited and many clinicians request supervision. Inexperienced mental health professionals might benefit from weekly sessions, while others, with more years of therapeutic work, do well with biweekly or monthly sessions. The supervisees rotate their case presentation, choosing a client about whose treatment they have concerns. The supervisor leads the group discussion. Here the type of supervision varies from directive to expert style with the less experienced clinicians and will be more consultative with the experienced clinicians (see chapter 1). All the supervisees participate in the discussion of the psychodynamics revealed or suggested by the case material and the interactions between therapist and patient.

Many mental health professionals have had little to no training in psychodynamics and psychotherapy principles. They often find themselves working in situations where such knowledge is either expected, necessary, or both. If they have had any psychotherapy experience, it is usually in one of the manualized therapies, most often cognitive-behavioral therapy. As in the examples given at the beginning of chapter 1, these clinicians can become overwhelmed by their experiences and may seek other employment or occasionally ask for supervision or consultation. Unfortunately, there are difficulties in obtaining such assistance, as outlined in the previous chapter. Many employers will not offer supervision opportunities to their clinicians who then have to decide whether to seek this personally. Expense and time constraints then add to the complexity of finding a supervisor.

Furthermore, many mental health clinicians are unaware of extensive research demonstrating the efficacy of the psychotherapies.[1,2] Thus, they are unable or unwilling to advocate for training in a psychotherapy. Consultation about a clinical problem where a client seems to be demonstrating refractory symptoms or noncompliance can lead to a discussion with a more psychologically minded clinician that clarifies the underlying psychodynamics of the patient or of the clinical interaction. This may then lead to requests for more such sessions and a growing interest in psychodynamics and psychological treatments.

### Clinical Example

As a psychotherapist known to have had experience with people who had been sexually abused, I was asked to provide a workshop for a city's community sexual assault clinic's staff. The stated purpose was to assist liaisons between the different services available in that city, to mediate some resultant disputes, and to increase the exchange of information between services. The workshop began with the presentation of a case of sexual assault and the difficulties the presenting clinician was encountering in trying to assist her client. The discussion soon revolved around psychosocial aspects and, later, transference and countertransference issues. The clinic's staff had little to no formal psychological training and rudimentary counseling skills. It became obvious that the problems between services in that community were driven by the frustrations arising from such lack of clinical experience. The staff's resultant feelings of inadequacy in helping their clients were projected on other agencies.

The workshop clarified the need for more education and clinical support for these beleaguered clinicians who were struggling to assist their clients. In turn, it was then possible to address the problems with interagency cooperation without rancor. The agency sponsoring the workshop undertook to arrange further training for a number of key individuals in each of the services.

## SEMINARS

### Occasional

Inviting mental health clinicians to attend a seminar sponsored by an umbrella organization is another type of group setting for supervision/consultation. Here a consultant with expertise in psychodynamic psychotherapy is engaged to facilitate the seminar. The day begins with a lecture on a topic previously identified as relevant to the clinical work of the professionals attending, such as managing self-harming patients. A case presentation by an attendee is then utilized to discuss the management problem from a psychodynamic perspective. This is followed by a description of psychotherapeutic approaches to the patient and further discussion tailored to the experience level of the participants. This approach is especially useful when the attendees have differing backgrounds in the mental health professions. As noted previously, many working in mental health services have little to no training in psychodynamic treatment modalities. Practically, such seminars can introduce a large number of clinicians to psychodynamic concepts and interest them in obtaining further training and supervision.

Following one such series of seminars, the participants were asked to comment on the usefulness of the sessions. They came from a variety of professional backgrounds, and most had minimal to no psychotherapy training. All had chosen to attend either because they recognized that they were having difficulties dealing with such clients or because they were finding interagency cooperation problematic in trying to assist these clients. The responses to the seminar format were uniform: all liked the lecture–case discussion format. They felt that they benefited from a case-based learning approach. The link between theory and practice made in this type of format was practical for them and provided a basis of understanding clients that had not been there previously. The opportunity to discuss case management experiences was seen as encouraging. They asked for more such sessions in order to learn in detail about recognized psychological treatments. Finally, they felt that their own efforts in their workplaces were being confirmed as valuable because management had allowed them time to attend the seminar(s).

While not a traditional type of supervision, this method introduces mental health staff to psychodynamic concepts and the utility of psychotherapy treatment. The seminar emphasizes the role of supervision and peer consultation in patient care and management and encourages the participants to seek such assistance with their clinical work.

## Scheduled

### *Large Group*

Here clinical staff have requested supervision be available in the workplace or the administration has recognized the need for supervision. Because of time limitations due to workload demands or because of financial constraints, supervision is arranged for a group of personnel at one time on a regular basis. The case discussion can be around one case continuously or a new case at each session in a rotation. The supervisory method will be determined by the expertise of the participant clinicians. Just as in all supervision, at times the supervisor may move flexibly between a consultative and a directive role, depending on the clinical situation.

In such group sessions with regular attendees as supervisees, the supervisor must be aware of group dynamics in addition to the concerns about trust and shame mentioned previously. If the supervisor comes from another, separate clinical location or agency, issues of confidentiality and trust in the workplace between supervisor and supervisee are minimized. However, the participants' fear of exposure to colleagues must be dealt with as part of the supervisory group process. The supervisor's attitude of acceptance, respect for each person's capabilities, and collegiality will help minimize feelings of shame and mistrust amongst the coworkers in this group. The supervisees participate actively in the discussion, and ideas are heard and discussed within a psychodynamic framework. At times, active management issues must be considered during the session in addition to psychotherapeutic approaches, techniques, impasses, and progress. The quality of the therapeutic alliance in each case is a focus, while transference and countertransference aspects are also considered.

One such supervision group completed open-ended questionnaires after one year of monthly sessions with the same supervisor. The replies were unidentifiable and spontaneous, but the content was consistent, and these repeated comments are quoted here. All respondents found the supervision sessions to be clinically helpful and asked that they continue. The factors found to be useful centered on improvement in their clinical skills. They found that the supervision sessions helped "to put things in perspective" and gave "alternate ways to approach problems." They felt that this was accomplished through learning "to understand own and client's reactions," learning "to recognize transference and countertransference issues," and developing "recognition of psychological processes."

As a result, they wrote that supervision was helping them "to avoid making the same mistakes over and over again." The sessions were seen "to reduce anxiety" about their clinical work and to encourage them to "remain within the treatment plan and not get sidetracked." In addition, supervision "ensured that our clients are getting the best possible practice."

The large majority had not had previous supervision in psychodynamic psychotherapy. A few had had supervision in cognitive-behavioral therapy. Most had had little education or training in psychological theories or psychotherapies, though all had mental health professional qualifications. They worked in busy inner-city community clinics and outreach programs and had large caseloads. They had regular clinical supervision in the workplace, but this focused only on management issues.

All of those who had had unsatisfactory psychotherapy supervision previously stated that the lack of satisfaction derived from mistrust of the supervisor. These supervisees perceived their respective earlier supervisors in each instance as "punitive," and therefore "I couldn't raise circumstances, which I was finding difficult. I didn't trust the supervisor."

### *Small Group*

When supervisors are difficult to find or have limited time available, clinicians may ask to be supervised along with another or other colleagues. Usually these professionals know each other and are comfortable with joint supervision. Still, the supervisor has to be aware of the same issues of trust, shame, and competition among the supervisees. Care must be taken to ensure that each professional has attention paid to his or her clinical concerns. Having cases presented in rotation best accomplishes this. Clinicians who practice in different settings can be supervised together when the supervision centers on psychodynamic theories and psychotherapy. In the final three chapters of this volume, this type of supervision is discussed from the supervisees' perspective.

## A SUPERVISOR'S EXPERIENCES

Here I describe and discuss experiences I have had as a supervisor in a variety of clinical situations. My concept of supervision is as described by Alonso:

> The supervisor is focused primarily on the clinical and professional development of the supervisee. Thus, the supervisor is always perched on the border between teaching the student and therapeutically addressing the implicit developmental impediments in the student's learning. The supervisor, in effect, must listen with a clinician's ear and speak with a teacher's mouth. (55)[3]

Becoming a supervisor ideally should involve specific training, as described in chapter 5. However, this training is frequently unavailable in most communities. Instead, as described in chapter 1, often an experienced clinician is asked by another professional for a consultation or supervision on the basis of knowledge of the clinical work of the former. At times, the request may be for supervision in psychodynamic psychotherapy but often begins as assistance with a management problem. As all mental health treatment benefits from a psychosocial understanding of the patient/client and from an appreciation of the interaction between client and professional, such assistance can rapidly move to a psychodynamic focus. Even psychopharmacological treatment is dependent on compliance, and compliance is directly correlated to the therapeutic relationship. Integrated, split, or joint treatment of a patient by two professionals can be negatively affected by a lack of appreciation of the psychodynamic factors involved.

These issues may become apparent to the supervisor during the presentation of the case. For example, a mental health professional presented a case of a client with a multitude of complaints—physical, psychological, and social—for a group supervision session as a management problem. It quickly was evident that the presenter, as case manager, had a strong positive alliance with the client, while others in the treatment team did not and were questioning the time the professional spent with this individual. The presenter had little training in psychodynamic theory or treatments and was providing counseling on a weekly basis to this client. As a result, the client's hospitalizations had been very significantly reduced, as had her use of auxiliary mental health services.

The supervisor focused on the psychological development of the client in terms of attachment and object relationships. The importance to the treatment of the need to understand the issues underlying the person's behaviors was emphasized. Discussion then centered on the effect of these issues on the client's interactions with mental health and social services. Conflicts between the team members over the treatment of the client then became evident and were clarified and openly discussed. Finally, the concepts of transference and countertransference were described by the supervisor, followed by an examination of their role in this case. All the supervisees participated in the discussions as the session moved back and forth between teaching psychodynamic concepts by the supervisor, examination of the relevance of these in this particular case by the entire group, and consideration of management and treatment.

As the sessions with a group like this continue, the participants are able to use their increasing knowledge of psychodynamics and psychotherapeutic treatments to become more active in the discussions, while the supervisor, in turn, becomes more consultative and less a teacher of basic theory. The case presentations begin to contain more psychodynamic content rather than being a recitation of events and descriptions of clinical impasses.

In my experience, it is important when supervising a group to keep psychodynamic psychotherapy experiential levels fairly similar. Problems occur when some supervisees in such a group situation are far less experienced than others. Either the more knowledgeable are bored when the level is elementary, or the less trained are bewildered when knowledge is assumed. In each instance, supervisees withdraw from the group.

Another occurrence that can be problematic is the entrance of a new supervisee to a well-established group. This is especially so with a small group and reflects any group process. While the group here exists for supervision, group processes are still of importance and can interfere with the supervision itself. The supervisor then may be working both as supervisor and as group leader. The supervisory session can founder on group dynamics unless these are recognized and dealt with by the supervisor and the group.

For example, two clinicians had been meeting monthly with a supervisor. They asked to have a colleague join the group. The new person had difficulty finding a comfortable role; the other two supervisees, though superficially welcoming, were not allowing her to intrude on their interactions with the supervisor. They became impatient with her presentations and appeared not to be interested when she spoke. Her psychotherapeutic skills were basic, and the others clearly did not wish to assist her progress despite inviting her into the sessions. The situation resolved only when she left to form another small group with the same supervisor.

Interventions by the supervisor were unsuccessful with the original group, as the interpersonal dynamics originated before the group began and were not primary to the supervisory process itself. The supervisor was not aware of this situation before the third person joined the group. It appeared that the invitation to partake in the group was an unconscious effort by the two clinicians to make the third aware of her need for supervision.

In a review of studies of therapists' skills, Eells wrote,

> Therapeutic mastery is not simply a matter of accumulated experience doing therapy, but involves constant engagement in improving skills, gaining new knowledge, and remaining open to experience and feedback from others. (317)[4]

For a supervisor-therapist, working with experienced clinicians can result in collegiality and be a learning experience for the supervisor. The supervisor must remain current and aware of recent literature and stay focused on supervision tasks, as collegiality can tempt one to allow a session to become more one of peer review than one of supervision. As in all supervision, there must be an emphasis on confidentiality, learning, and mutual respect.

This delineation is especially important in a small "community," that is, when supervisor and supervisees have frequent contact outside of supervision sessions because of geographical proximity, mutual interests, organizational and professional activities, and/or social events. Supervision must remain within the sessions, much as therapy does not take place outside formal psychotherapy sessions.

When supervisory resources are limited, problems may arise that are similar to what can occur when mental health professionals practice in a small community. These difficulties can arise even in large urban centers, for example, when few psychotherapists are available or willing to supervise, when a limited number of external supervisors are known to clinicians who all work together, or when professional associations or programs bring clinicians together. In such instances, professionals may discover that they have a supervisor in common with coworkers. This can arouse concerns about confidentiality, influence, and favoritism. The supervisor may be unaware of the connection between supervisees, much as can happen with patients. However, because of the nature of supervision's removal from personal psychotherapy for the supervisee, the supervisor may not be told about these concerns. Future appointments are canceled without explanation, and the supervision ends. Here the line between supervision and psychotherapy has placed a barrier to the supervisory process. This disruption is, in my experience, more likely to occur when supervision is new or when the workplace is in turmoil.

The externally based supervisor may not be aware of the workplace rivalries or disruptions between particular staff members. Often the discussion of clinical issues does not include the use of names of individuals as part of the confidential nature of the supervisory process, or the supervisee does not reveal that there are conflicts with particular colleagues over the treatment being offered to that client. The task is to assist the supervisee to learn how to resolve clinical situations and therapeutic and technical problems, not to learn the details of other professionals. Thus, the supervisor may not know or discern that another supervisee is involved in the issue being discussed. Once again, the supervisor employs the skills of a therapist and the attitude of a teacher, as stated previously. Concerns about confidentiality should be discussed as part of the process, as trust is as essential a part of supervision as it is of therapy. Ideally, supervisory impasses would lead to consultation with other supervisors when such are available.

Here too there is a difference between supervision of clinicians and trainees. Trainees are usually assigned supervisors, and avenues are in place through which to resolve any perceived problems in the supervisory relationship. In contrast, clinician supervision is often voluntary and can be discontinued easily. Despite recognizing that the professional's skills are such that supervision is needed, the supervisor can only attempt to resolve any reluctance to continue by the supervisee. Unlike working with a patient, however, here the therapist can use only therapeutic techniques, not personal information, in this effort. The development of a supervisory alliance, in these instances, requires therapeutic skills, and the process itself can reveal much about the supervisee's interpersonal style that affects his or her treatment of clients. In chapter 3, a discussion by a psychoanalyst of supervision of trainees and beginning therapists in psychodynamic psychotherapy further elucidates these points.

## TOOLS

In either individual or group supervision settings, the supervisor and supervisee(s) can utilize a variety of tools, just as in supervision of trainees. These include detailed notes of each treatment session, a summary of the session, videotape, or recorded tape. Video- and teleconferencing for long-distance supervision is useful for those clinicians unable to obtain supervision in the area in which they reside and practice. While videotapes, in my experience, provide the most accurate record of an interaction between professional and patient, the equipment needed is usually not available in practice settings. Some find the filming to be intrusive and fear that it will alter the therapeutic relationship or impede the patient's revelations. When used, the patients, in my experience, are more accepting than the clinicians of the presence of the recording camera. Videotaping also produces more material than can be used during a supervisory hour but does allow for the viewing of excerpts that can elucidate the dynamics of the therapy. It is an extremely valuable method for the supervision of beginning trainees who can also look at the video sessions self-critically.

Detailed notes are most helpful in the supervision of those with little training or practice experience and, like videotapes, allow the supervisee the opportunity to review the session before discussing it with the supervisor. However, the writing of the notes can interfere with the interaction between the clinician and the patient. Some are too preoccupied with note taking to pay adequate attention to the therapeutic interaction. The constant writing may equally distract the patient.

Most professionals present a summary of the session to the supervisor. Those with more knowledge about psychotherapy and psychodynamics either usually focus on particular issues with which they are having problems or present a troublesome clinical case to the supervisor. In other instances, a case presentation and review of the treatment sessions can prompt a number of questions from the supervisor in order to elucidate the therapeutic impasse(s). The supervision then proceeds in either a directive or a collaborative mode (see chapter 1), depending on the therapeutic sophistication of the supervisee.

## SUPERVISION OR CONSULTATION

Some of the descriptions given here of supervision might also be seen as consultation between colleagues. Consultation is often used to obtain a second opinion on a diagnosis or treatment approach. Sometimes it is a means to terminate treatment and to refer the patient elsewhere. Supervision, on the other hand, involves an exchange between a more experienced clinician and one who is trying to learn more about a treatment method. Therefore, supervision can be brief or continue over a number of sessions. Supervision with clinicians is conceptualized differently from the supervision of a trainee in any of the mental health professions because evaluation to meet the standards and requirements of a program for a mental health profession is not part of the process. Gabbard writes,

> The effective use of supervision during one's training year sets the tone for ongoing consultation throughout one's professional life. Therapists should develop an attitude that they do not have to solve every problem on their own. Even if therapists have their own personal treatment experience—which is extraordinarily helpful in dynamic therapy—they will still have blind spots. Consultants who are not immersed in the heat of the transference-countertrans-

> ference dynamics bring an outside perspective to the dyad that is enormously valuable when one is stuck at an impasse with a patient. (184–85)[5]

The chapters that follow discuss many of the points made in the first two chapters in more detail. Chapter 3, on the supervision of trainees in psychodynamic psychotherapy by a psychoanalyst, describes the process of supervision in more detail, and these descriptions can be applied to supervision with all clinicians. Chapter 4 discusses topics often ignored or avoided in both supervision and treatment but topics that are very relevant to both interactions between individuals and those related to gender, ethnicity, and culture. Chapter 5 outlines training programs for supervisors, and suggestions are given for improving supervisory skills. Chapter 6 deals with the important area of boundary violations, an important topic for all mental health professionals. The last three chapters form a section in which three practicing psychiatrists write about their experiences with supervision and consultation. Although these chapters are written by psychiatrists, their personal and professional descriptions are applicable to all clinicians.

## NOTES

1. Falk Leichsenring, Sven Rabung, and Eric Leibing, "The Efficacy of Short-Term Psychodynamic Psychotherapy in Specific Psychiatric Disorders: A Meta-Analysis," *Archives of General Psychiatry* 61 (2004): 1208–16.
2. Anthony Roth and Peter Fonagy, *What Works for Whom? A Critical Review of Psychotherapy Research* (New York: Guilford Press, 1996).
3. Anne Alonso, "On Being Skilled and Deskilled as a Psychotherapy Supervisor," *Journal of Psychotherapy Practice and Research* 9 (2000): 55–61.
4. Tracey D. Eells, "What Do We Know about Master Therapists?," *Journal of Psychotherapy Practice and Research* 8 (1999): 314–17.
5. Glen O. Gabbard, *Long-Term Psychodynamic Psychotherapy: A Basic Text* (Washington, D.C.: American Psychiatric Publishing, 2004), 173–87.

# II

# ISSUES IN SUPERVISION AND CONSULTATION IN PSYCHODYNAMIC PSYCHOTHERAPY

# 3

# Supervising Psychodynamic Psychotherapy

*Norman A. Clemens*

Supervising psychodynamic psychotherapy is more than a teaching exercise because psychodynamic psychotherapy is more than a cognitive experience. The supervisor must be attuned to the affective tone of the therapeutic interaction as well as to the unfolding relationship between the therapist and the patient. These in turn provide indications of the hidden agendas—the less-than-conscious elements of mental life in both parties. Beyond that, these agendas may be reflected in the interaction between the therapist and the supervisor. The supervisor's skills as a therapist are called into play, yet the supervision must not become a therapy in its own right.

The hallmark of psychodynamic psychotherapy is individualization of the therapy to the uniqueness of each patient. Rather than categorizing patients rigidly, the psychodynamic approach views the entire person in a framework that helps to identify and understand not only the presenting symptoms but also the developmental, biological, and environmental variables that have shaped that person's personality and the manner in which these variables contribute to the present clinical situation. These assessments in turn guide the approach to treatment, and they are subject to revision as knowledge of the patient deepens.

Furthermore, the assessments intersect with an array of psychoanalytic theoretical constructions that provide a selection of frameworks for understanding—topographical theory, drive theory, ego psychology, object relations theory, self psychology, attachment theory, intersubjectivity theory, and newly identified neuropsychological–neurobiological correlations—to name just the most prominent. Supervision of a nascent therapist or, for that matter, consultation with an experienced colleague calls for the supervisor's familiarity with all of these levels of variability in order to augment the therapist's acuity and sensitivity in skillfully working with the patient. Although manuals for subtypes of psychodynamic psychotherapy exist, the basic pleomorphism of psychodynamic psychotherapy sets it apart from therapies that can be reduced to a highly structured manual that lends itself to a simple instructional process. Supervision of psychodynamic psychotherapy is a clinical encounter.

Although psychoanalytic theory and a century of clinical experience inform psychodynamic psychotherapy, psychodynamic psychotherapy is not simply a modified form of psychoanalysis. *Psychoanalysis* as a treatment method has

1. a structured treatment framework that has been found to facilitate
2. fundamental psychoanalytic processes in the treatment relationship (transference and countertransference) and
3. access to unconscious mental life (free association, use of dreams, fantasies, behaviors, and so on).

These allow

4. deeper awareness of developmental processes going back to childhood and
5. of current inner psychic conflict, defense mechanisms, self-representations, and object relations (intrapsychic representations of relationships with other people),
6. which in turn bring about change (probably in neural networks as well as thought patterns) through intense, repetitive mental experiences (working through).

For a variety of reasons, *psychodynamic psychotherapy* is not designed to achieve that degree of breadth or intensity of mental experience, insight, or change. The methods and goals are related but generally modified. Because individual patients, therapists, and clinical situations vary widely, however, the results of the two forms of therapy are not necessarily so widely divergent as this description would imply. Some psychoanalyses do not achieve a full psychoanalytic process, and some psychotherapy patients do achieve a therapeutic experience and clinical results comparable to analysis. Nonetheless, psychodynamic psychotherapy is usually seen as a treatment method in its own right rather than a modified form of psychoanalysis.

## THE SUPERVISORY FRAME

Supervision should be a collegial experience between two mutually respected therapists. The "frame" of psychodynamic supervision bears some resemblance to the treatment frame. It is private, and the contents of clinical discussions are confidential, including personal disclosures by the supervisee. In training situations, multispecialty practices, or clinics, the supervisor may have a responsibility to report to overseers the results of any evaluation of the supervisee's work but only within an ambit of respect for the supervisee's personal privacy and the confidentiality of the patient.

In most supervisory situations, there is a power differential arising either from a training environment or from the supervisor's role as a considerably more experienced colleague with a higher status. The supervisee's self-confidence and self-esteem are vulnerable. Supervisees are entitled to respect, tact, professionalism, and freedom from harsh or demeaning criticism on the part of the supervisor. Ethical standards of the professions that practice psychotherapy commonly forbid supervisors from engaging in sexual or exploitative relationships with supervisees.[1] Supervision is generally scheduled at regular intervals for a specified length of time, the participants are prompt, the setting is private, and the time is protected from casual cancellations; distractions, such as working over lunch; or nonemergent interruptions, such as telephone calls or other people entering the room. Arrangements such as fee structure, mode of operation, or responsibilities for reporting about the therapist's work to a training program are well understood at the outset.

Therapists learn a great deal by patterning their behavior on the model demonstrated by supervisors, especially early in their careers. The way in which the supervisor establishes the frame of supervision may substantially influence the therapist's mode of setting the frame for therapies they conduct. Supervisees often identify with their supervisors, for better or worse, and much of this occurs with little awareness in the realm of procedural memory. Because of the ubiquitous defense mechanism of turning passive into active, a supervisor's failure to maintain a frame of supervision, ranging from inconsiderate to seductive or abusive behavior, may be highly detrimental to supervisees' future conduct of therapeutic relationships with their patients.

**Case example:** A supervisee admitted being consistently late in starting sessions with his patient, to which she responded with recurrent feelings of hurt and anger. The supervisor realized that she was frequently late in starting supervisory sessions and pointed this out to the supervisee. Both supervisor and therapist acknowledged their disrespectful behavior and the likelihood that the therapist was turning passive into active rather than to express his feelings to the supervisor. They made an effort to be prompt in future sessions, allowing the patient to deal with her long-standing issues of feeling inferior and poorly treated.

Early idealization of the supervisor in a supervision that is going well may gradually evolve into the supervisee's more realistic awareness of the supervisor's human traits, and eventually the learning therapist develops autonomy and his or her own individual style of working. So in the master–apprentice relationship does the apprentice become a master.

## KNOWING WHAT IS GOING ON IN THE THERAPY

Supervisors yearn to know what is *really* happening in the therapy. "Perfection" in this regard would entail the supervisor's being invisibly present in the room and telepathically knowing the supervisee's every observation, emotion, hypothesis about the material that is emerging, random thoughts, and associations—as well as making direct, independent observations of the patient—and it would in no way intrude on the treatment process. Obviously—and fortunately—this idealized option is not only internally inconsistent but also impossible. Supervised therapists should have their own space in which to practice their own skills and form unalloyed therapeutic relationships, and the supervisor enters this space at the invitation of the therapist.

Failing the foregoing fantastical proposition, there are a number of avenues for knowing what is going on, each with its own advantages and disadvantages:

1. The supervisor may be present in the room, as unobtrusively as possible. This permits the most complete observation that is achievable, but it intrudes on the therapy by putting an additional person in the room, which the patient may in time accept. However, the patient's transference fantasies and feelings will include the supervisor, and this will have to be reckoned with. The presence of the supervisor presents the therapist in an obvious subordinate status. It also calls on the supervisor for additional time outside of supervisory sessions. Nonetheless, there may be times when an occasional session with the supervisor present may be especially helpful—perhaps in a crisis, with an inexperienced therapist, or when direct observation or evaluation of the patient's clinical state is desirable because it is not being communicated well enough in reports. When it is obvious that a struggling therapist is working under

supervision, the appearance of the supervisor may be reassuring and demystifying for the patient.

2. The supervisor may observe the sessions through a one-way window or on videotape. Although this is less of a direct intrusion by the supervisor, the patient must be informed of the observation, which adds an element of mysterious, unseen presence that also will affect the patient's and the therapist's fantasies and emotions. It has the same drawbacks affecting the therapist's status and the supervisor's time as the preceding option. It also does not let the supervisor in on what the therapist is thinking or feeling except for subtle, observable clues.
3. Audiotaped recordings present a similar dilemma minus the visual observations.
4. "Verbatim" process notes are seldom truly verbatim, but detailed notes can convey considerable information about the treatment, including the therapist's internal reactions, self-observations, strategic thinking, and commentary along the way. The supervisee has to supply the affective elements and rationale while reading or discussing the notes. Listening to a droning recital of detailed notes can be tedious and mind-numbing; some supervisors read them in advance of the meeting with the supervisee. Accuracy and completeness must essentially be compromised because the therapist will have to rely on memory while writing notes after the treatment session, which may take as much time as the session itself and will nonetheless be subject to defensive lapses of memory. Taking detailed notes during therapy sessions—in an effort to improve accuracy and save time—is severely distracting to the therapist and probably to the patient as well, and it impedes the freedom and spontaneity of the therapist's associations and anticipation of responses; for these reasons, I strongly discourage such a practice.
5. Using sketchier notes to prompt the supervisee's spontaneous recollections and thoughts about the work during the supervisory hour makes for a livelier supervision session and more insight into the supervisee's creative thinking and countertransference responses. Detail is sacrificed, and it is easier for the therapist to defensively exclude important material than in detailed notes written right after the treatment session. I prefer some combination of this option with the preceding one, depending on the nature of the treatment, the therapist's level of experience and skill, and other variables that may change as the supervision progresses.
6. The supervisee may unconsciously reveal aspects of the work through slips or reenactments in the supervisory sessions. Arlow[2] describes a supervisee who was concerned about a change in the patient that he could not clearly characterize; the supervisee's manner of speaking became uncharacteristically very pressured and excited, of which he

> was unaware until the supervisor pointed it out. At this point he realized that he was talking as his patient had and that she was becoming hypomanic. Other supervisees may become provocative, withholding, argumentative, seductive, or any of a myriad of behaviors that reveal an identification with a patient.

Bernstein[3] has devised a system of notating psychoanalytic work that combines alternating modes of presenting selected detailed material ("the experiencing section"), commentary ("the reflecting section"), and interval summaries ("a transitional narrative"). Training centers often require a periodic summary that presents an overview of what has transpired in the psychoanalytic work during that interval.

Note keeping for supervisory purposes differs from documentation for administrative or legal purposes because of the intimate, personal nature of the material that is relevant to psychodynamic psychotherapy. While a general clinical record contains descriptive information from history, examination, laboratory findings, and so on that is the foundation of legal responsibility, detailed process material belongs in psychotherapy notes—a separate part of the medical record as defined by the privacy regulations issued under the Health Insurance Portability and Accountability Act of 1996 (HIPAA)—or in completely deidentified personal working notes of the therapist, to be destroyed after their purpose has been served.[4]

## ACHIEVING AN EMPATHIC CONNECTION

Beyond knowing what is going on in the therapy—and more challenging—is reaching the point where the supervisor feels a sense of knowing the patient as a person, grasping his or her inner conflicts and distress, sensing the process that is occurring between the patient and the therapist, and integrating all of this in a way close to what one experiences when one is in tune with one's own patient. This kind of a "feel" for the patient and the therapeutic process stays with the supervisor and reduces the reliance on notes to restore a mental image of the therapy from one supervisory session to the next. How quickly this is achieved can vary widely, depending on the patient and the supervisee's ability to communicate his or her own "feel" for the patient, but it usually requires a few supervisory sessions at least. Less frequent supervisory sessions make it more difficult. In the following case example, this sense of being in tune was achieved in an unusual fashion.

> **Case example:** I was having continuing difficulty getting a sense of empathic attunement with the patient and a feel for what was happening in the therapy. The supervisee, an advanced psychiatric resident, was

doing better at reporting what was taking place in the sessions, and the fact that the patient continued in the treatment seemed like an encouraging development for this supervisee. Nonetheless, I felt as if I had to get reacquainted with the case every time we met.

About ten minutes into a supervisory session, the resident suddenly expressed chagrin that he had left in his car a sheaf of notes that the patient had written to him between several recent sessions and given to him. With amusement in his voice, he said, "Do you suppose leaving them in the car was resistance?" "Perhaps," I responded. "Let's consider that as we go along." (I was delighted that he had become open enough to considering countertransference processes to raise the question.) He went on to describe the sessions, which were showing signs of getting beyond her florid somatic symptoms and constricting anxieties to some underlying feelings. Near the end of the supervisory session, which was at the end of my working day, I suggested that he go out to his car and retrieve the notes she had written.

They turned out to be remarkable, and I stayed overtime to read them. They were daily journals, beginning with a timetable of the occurrence of symptoms, followed by a narrative of what had gone through her mind that day. Of note was the fact that her handwriting shifted from a rounded, childlike style to a more slanted script as each note went along. Early notes were full of mounting anxiety and somatic symptoms, coupled with helpless despair about a life situation that was deteriorating into poverty and even possible homelessness. As they evolved, there were several references to the way in which her thoughts got going after sessions, and she became aware of things she had not recognized before. She began to relate feelings about the breakup of her marriage seven years before, how shabbily her ex-husband had treated her with flaunting a new love relationship and cutting off financial support, and how she had fallen from a comfortable life situation as a suburban housewife rearing her children to being alone in poverty, neglected by her sons, and prevented by her phobic symptoms from seeking work. It was a kind of "eureka!" moment for me, as the patient came alive through her own words. I was also impressed that an active therapeutic process was taking place after all, different from her previous rounds with residents who mostly renewed her medications: she was engaged in exploring her grief and anger in a way that might eventually lead to her being enabled to use her strengths, take charge of her life, and escape the current state of helpless paralysis. How much of this was due to the resident's development or the structure of the therapy itself was unclear, but perhaps the former was indicated by a comment of the resident, novel for him, as we discussed the notes: "As I read the notes I felt sad for her."

## DEALING WITH THE THERAPIST'S EMOTIONAL RESPONSES

Above all, in any mode of reporting, it is crucial that the supervisor be attuned not only to the events of the therapy but also to the emotional attributes of the sessions and the therapist's responses in the therapy, in supervision, and in inner life. The most distinctive dimension of psychodynamic psychotherapy that sets it apart from most other modes of therapy is the close attention to the relationship between patient and therapist. This relationship is seen as a prime source of learning about the patient's underlying psychological processes and the developmental history that brought them about. The partnership that develops is a *working alliance*, devoted to understanding and resolving the patient's problems. It is also the here-and-now stage on which problematic issues can be worked out, gradually building new associative and neural networking patterns. Using the acumen of therapeutic experience, the supervisor becomes aware of the subtleties of the therapist–patient relationship. Sometimes the supervisee reports them—more observantly, it is hoped, as he or she becomes more experienced. Often they show up in emotional asides or cues of which the therapist is not fully aware. A pattern in the relationship may take months to develop to the point where it becomes identifiable and can be traced to its roots.

Psychoanalytic thinking has increasingly focused on the interaction between therapist and patient, not as an imbalanced relationship in which the therapist studies the patient as an object but as an "intersubjective," shared experience in which both parties' roles and interactive psychic processes are scrutinized and learned from. A modern therapist might be more likely to reveal his or her own emotions in the treatment situation in order to facilitate mutual understanding of what is happening between them, although extensive personal disclosure or use of the patient to ventilate or work out one's own personal problems remains inappropriate.

At times, developments in the therapy manifest themselves in supervision through what is called "parallel process"—the reenactment in the supervisory relationship of something that is going on in the therapeutic relationship. This is not surprising since the supervisory relationship is also a continuing, highly charged interaction between two people to which both actively contribute regardless of the inequality of status. In most situations the supervisor is viewed as an expert and potentially helpful adviser and teacher but also as potentially critical and judging authority. Regardless of their level of experience, both supervisee and supervisor bring a degree of narcissistic vulnerability, a concern about how the other will view oneself and whether one's performance will be found satisfactory. This has even been compared to stage fright.[5] Competitive and exhibitionistic strivings may enter in, with various defenses against them. More will be said about this later.

Every therapist has a spectrum of emotional responses to patients—pleasure, admiration, or affection in working with some and envy, annoyance, anxiety, or boredom with others. To some degree the therapist is simply reacting to the patient as another person, similarly to the responses the patient evokes with people in general or the therapist habitually experiences with that kind of person because of their character structure. These are part of the working relationship between two personalities in a professional setting. An occasional patient might very closely resemble an important person in the therapist's early development, and if it is too difficult to keep them apart in one's feelings, it may be best to advise the supervisee to help them find another therapist. Supervision should help the therapist be more attuned to these emotional responses and to deal with them appropriately.

As the treatment relationship deepens, there may be increasing evidence in supervision that the patient is developing feelings and interactions with the therapist that are less than appropriate to the current situation but resemble those in past important relationships, known as *transference* into the present treatment relationship.[6] Such developments are at first largely unconscious. The therapist may discern them after they have become recognizable as a pattern, or the supervisor may notice the pattern while the therapist is still too close to the scene to get the picture, or it may show up in a subtle change in the supervisory relationship. The supervisor may identify the transference pattern directly or pull together the relevant observations in a way that the supervisee can make the final step of identifying it. It then becomes a matter of judgment, timing, tact, and strategy to know if, when, and how the therapist should bring it to the patient's attention.

Similarly, the therapist may find that the treatment process has evoked a *countertransference* echoing his or her past important relationships, which must be recognized in supervision, acknowledged, and dealt with.[7, 8] (The concept of countertransference is sometimes applied broadly to refer to any feeling the therapist has about the patient, but the original concept more narrowly views it as the therapist's transference from his or her own developmental relationships; I favor the latter perspective. Originally, countertransference was viewed primarily as an obstruction to the therapy, but now its value in contributing to a two-person treatment process has been recognized.) The supervisory relationship becomes especially important here to enable freedom to discuss countertransference without fear of being judged, criticized, or demeaned, although limits on behavior with the patient may have to be worked out. Supervision helps differentiate between impulse and thought on the one hand and behavior on the other. By bringing the countertransference to light, it may be constructively managed to advance the treatment. At this juncture it is especially crucial that the distinction between supervision and therapy be respected; exploration of the personal underpinnings of the supervisee's countertransference belongs elsewhere, in personal therapy or self-analysis.

**Case example:** An experienced therapist reported in supervision that she was feeling highly resentful and indignant in response to a patient's reports of his bullying his early teenaged son. This was making it difficult to engage him in appreciating what he was doing to the boy and understanding what motivated him. In supervision she realized that her father had treated her in a similar fashion, while her older brother could do no wrong. Recognizing this countertransference allowed her to sort her personal feelings out from her relationship with the patient and proceed with therapeutic work.

Individual psychodynamic psychotherapies can be classified along a spectrum in which the extremes are *expressive* and *supportive*. Some degree of both elements is present in most therapies. Work with the transference takes place toward the expressive end of the spectrum, which bears more resemblance to psychoanalysis. In some psychotherapies, the psychodynamic psychotherapist may use a psychoanalytic model of mental life to help the patient understand current dynamic processes and relationships with other people in the environment rather than giving primary attention to the treatment relationship itself unless it is not going well. For example, the therapist may identify a defense the patient is using that affects a relationship outside the treatment setting and work with the patient to understand the unconscious threat that prompts the defense. Or the therapist may help the patient see behavior patterns that disrupt relationships with a spouse, a child, a boss, or a parent. Here the therapist is functioning as an ally or a guide for the patient in exploring his or her inner world as it relates to the social environment. There is a risk of such work becoming sterile, intellectualized, and nonmutative if the patient isolates from awareness the emotional aspects of these issues, but on the other hand it may be the only entrée into psychological understanding that a highly guarded patient may allow.

The supervisor may assist the therapist in understanding such aspects of the patient's life but nonetheless must be attuned to subtle elements of transference and countertransference that are developing unawares. As Douglas Bond used to remark during my training, "Transference is like mushrooms: it grows best in the dark."

At the most supportive end of the spectrum are sympathy, consolation, encouragement, suggestion, advice, or limit setting—interventions that limit exploration but may be appropriate or even advisable. The supervisor's role is to help the therapist sort out the rationale and strategy that guide the therapist in setting the tone of the therapy; his or her flexibility in the supervisory relationship may be a model for the supervisee in so doing.

## TEACHING MODES OF RESPONSE

Therapists can respond on many levels to the material the patient brings to sessions. Supervision can help them gauge what is appropriate to the present situation and what the patient is ready for. Often the therapist will simply *repeat* what the patient has said, which helps to fix it in memory and be less vulnerable to defensive repression. At other times the therapist may seek *clarification* and further elaboration through questioning or prompting by repeating certain words the patient has used. A more complex level of response is *confrontation* through gathering consciously stated elements of the conversation and the history in such a way that the mosaic of these elements demonstrates a pattern of which the patient was previously unaware. Less frequently the intervention rises to the level of an *interpretation*, in which the therapist goes beyond what has been revealed by the patient to address certain emerging insights that are unconscious at that moment but appear to be close to awareness (preconscious). The supervisor's role is to help the supervisee to be clear about what level of intervention is taking place and to develop clinical judgment about when and how to use them.

Often the intervention takes the form of identifying a *defense mechanism* the patient is using, working with the anxiety that underlies it, and helping the patient gain a new, more mature perspective on what was being defended against in order to avoid the anxiety. Supervision helps the therapist appreciate and understand how defense mechanisms operate, contributing the vantage point of a less involved, more objective third party and perhaps breaking a logjam that occurred because the patient and the therapist were too close to the material to see what was happening. What seemed like an impasse becomes an opening.

Experienced supervisors may suggest very tactful, well-attuned ways of phrasing an intervention that supervisees are tempted to write down laboriously and try to use verbatim. It is likely to work much better if the supervisee is helped to understand why the supervisor put it that way but to use his or her own words as they make sense in the actual situation of therapy. Occasional role playing may help the learning therapist develop these skills in his or her own style.

## PHASES OF DEVELOPMENT OF A PSYCHOTHERAPIST

The development of a psychotherapist runs through stages somewhat comparable to the stages of a completed psychotherapy, and supervision of a trainee evolves accordingly as the trainee progresses.[9] The pace of evolution of a psychotherapist varies, however, depending on the trainee's innate capabilities, interests, personality, cultural and educational background, and opportunities for clinical experience—as well as the quality of supervision and didactic instruction. Not all mental health professionals can be expected to evolve into highly effective psychodynamic therapists. Thus, it is my view that the expectations of "competence" to be reached during psychiatric residency training, according to the Psychiatric Residency Review Committee, have to be assessed on a relative scale. Few graduating psychiatric residents have fully reached their potential effectiveness in conducting psychodynamic psychotherapy, but many can do very well at it. For others, the minimum expectation would be that residents going on to other fields of psychiatry would know, understand, and respect the concepts and utility of psychodynamic psychotherapy. They should be able to take psychodynamic phenomena into account while evaluating and managing patients (even patients receiving other kinds of treatment), to recognize transference and countertransference, and to conduct psychodynamic psychotherapy when needed. This level of expertise would at least assure patients of added value in any kind of psychiatric encounter. Similar thoughts are relevant to the development of psychologists, social workers, and counselors.

## THE EVOLVING IDENTITY AS A THERAPIST

It takes years to feel like a really competent psychodynamic psychotherapist, most of the time. During the experiential process that leads to this sense of identity as a therapist, there are many adjustments to be made in one's sense of self and one's expectations and standards for oneself. Starting out as a therapist is hard work that, in my experience, gives one a sense of brain fatigue at the end of a long working day. Anxiety is high.[10] One's self-esteem and self-confidence are on the line, as in learning any challenging new skill and way of thinking, but perhaps more so because the experience is full of ambiguities, subtle unknowns, emotional pitfalls and intensities, and engagement of one's own psychic experience. Trainees with underlying narcissistic vulnerabilities may be especially at risk, but it is likely to be a challenging task for everyone.[11] Trainees begin with a very high expectation of themselves—an ego ideal that seeks perfection and a superego that may harshly criticize and punish any shortfall.[12, 13] Hoped-for therapeutic omnipotence, failing to materialize in the ups and downs of psychotherapy, may lead to feelings of impotence and failure, countertransference phenomena, and reenactment in the supervision—until it is replaced by a realistic sense of an imperfect, human, gradual process of understanding and incremental, modest change.

The stance of the supervisor is very important in helping trainees with these issues. Supervision is optimally an empathic, holding environment that is supportive and allows the trainee to express and contain feelings safely in relation to the therapy. The supervisor can acknowledge the anxiety that inevitably accompanies a new and challenging situation that calls for change in the new therapist's functioning and sense of self. The supervisor can validate the supervisee's ideas and emotional responses while helping him or her to deal with them constructively within a therapeutic framework and to be less self-critical about them. Identifications with the patient may show up in the supervision or be enacted in a parallel process within the supervision that also engages the supervisor. Sorting this out, including disclosure by the supervisor of his or her own responses within the supervisory process, becomes a learning experience in which the supervisee can identify with the supervisor's openness and valuing understanding over passing judgment. In this way, the internal experience of being a therapist gradually becomes part of the supervisee's identity.

## OPENING PHASE

In supervising the beginning psychotherapist, one must address the basics of the psychotherapeutic situation, just as these are fundamental to the initial stages of a therapy. The novice may not understand the rationale for an established time frame, regular intervals between sessions, punctuality, protection of privacy and confidentiality, avoidance of nonemergency interruptions by telephone calls or intrusions, and careful observance of professional and ethical boundaries. Besides explaining the rationale, the supervisor is responsible to assess whether these dimensions of the psychotherapeutic frame are being maintained and to help the therapist deal with any reasons why he or she finds it difficult to do so.

These structural arrangements become much more meaningful when the fledgling therapist becomes attuned to patients and to the relational experience of psychodynamic psychotherapy—to understand what it takes for patients to build enough trust in their therapist to reveal their innermost thoughts and feelings. Trainees can then understand the high priority given to creating a safe environment for psychodynamic psychotherapy, and they become aware of the privilege of having patients confide in them and sense a therapist's interest in their inner mental lives. The supervisees must also come to grips with their voyeuristic excitement in this new experience, along with the anxiety, attraction, revulsion, or urge to pass judgment they may feel at what they encounter. They must deal with the temptation to overidentify with the patient and lose the sense of the patient's unique individuality and autonomy. In the safe supervisory environment, they can acknowledge these natural feelings along with sorting out when their responses become problematic because of their own personal experiences.

Again, the supervisor must resist the temptation to become a therapist who explores underlying issues in the supervisee's life but rather can help identify patterns and problems, be supportive, and discuss what can be done about them.

A crucial skill that is especially important in psychodynamic work is being able to listen—to draw the patient out perhaps—but also to know how to wait, how to accept silences, and how to let the patients tell their stories in their own way and to be attuned to subtle cues and asides and know when and how to pursue them. The supervisor can model this skill in the supervisory sessions but also may have to provide instruction when the skill is lacking.

Initial rapport having been established, the supervisor guides the novice therapist in conducting a psychodynamically sensitive evaluation. A thorough assessment over several interviews garners not only the necessary clinical, descriptive information but also a personal narrative—emotionally relevant historical events often going back to childhood as well as inner conflicts, personality characteristics, important relationships, issues at home and work, and so on. This information is not accessible to checklists, stereotyped questioning, or a "just the facts!" approach. Nor is it reducible to a five-axis diagnosis of the *Diagnostic and Statistical Manual of Mental Disorders*. What should emerge is a picture of a person with a life story and a many-faceted present life situation. This in turn leads to a *psychodynamic formulation*, bringing to bear the therapist's understanding, based on theory and experience, of the patient's current dilemmas, strengths and vulnerabilities, adaptations and defensive patterns, interferences with phase-appropriate development, and the way these contribute to current symptoms and problematic behavior. There should also be an assessment of the patient's ability to relate appropriately to a therapist and his or her motivation and resources for treatment.

Unfortunately, other life circumstances may also intervene in a treatment decision, such as limited available time due to the patient's expectation of leaving town, limits on the therapist's span of working with the patient due to the end of a training period or anticipated departure from an agency, or financial limits imposed by third-party payers and/or limited income. These must be resolved in consultation with the patient, with the patient's best interests at heart.

This initial understanding of the patient's personality and problems is the basis of an individualized *psychodynamic treatment plan* proposing the format, emphasis, and focus of treatment. Concretely, how frequent and how long should sessions be? Should the therapy be more expressive and exploratory, or should it be more supportive? What specific goals can be provisionally agreed on between patient and therapist? Would the aim be to modify some underlying personality traits or to resolve a limited range of current conflicts and symptoms? How long would it be expected to take? Is there the basis of a constructive therapeutic relationship? Does the patient have the resources to see a therapy through to completion so as to avoid opening up issues that cannot be resolved in the time available? Should full-scale psychoanalysis be considered?

The supervisor's task is to think through these challenging questions with the supervisee. In the early stages of training, it is helpful for the trainee to write out such *formulations*, first in detail for didactic purposes and later in a more condensed way for documentation. There is no standard format except that the information and reasoning should proceed coherently and logically to the conclusions. If part of the patient's record, it should be in the more protected psychotherapy notes as defined by HIPAA. If third-party payers are involved and require a report on the rationale for psychotherapy, the supervisor may have to help the trainee draw on the formulation and treatment plan to create a "minimum necessary" summary in the main clinical record that respects the privacy of the patient's personal life and maintains confidentiality. Requisite communications with third parties may call for close supervision and the patient's approval of any information that leaves the treatment setting.

During the early phases of supervision, the supervisor may have to introduce many psychoanalytic concepts or reinforce what has been taught in didactic seminars. The supervision affords an opportunity to bring the drily intellectual theories to life through application to the real-life issues of a patient so that the trainee can begin to see their utility. While a didactic stance may be appropriate, the real value is in the clinical correlation with the trainee's experience.

Early on, the trainee must recognize and empathically address resistance by the patient (and perhaps by oneself) to a psychological, exploratory mode of dealing with the presenting issues, not exclusively focused on relieving symptoms. Building a therapeutic alliance must take that into account. It is the beginning of developing a more effective "observing ego." At this stage of therapy, it may call for some education about how therapy works. The supervisor can help the trainee respond empathically and constructively rather than be discouraged. Early trainees can resonate with what a mind-stretching experience it is to think in new ways about one's experiences and inner life.

## MIDDLE PHASE

Once the treatment is under way, the supervisor tracks the evolution of the work through the means discussed earlier. The task is to help the supervisee detect the nuances that open up understanding of the problem and help devise strategies for communicating with the patient in a way that broadens the patient's understanding and mastery. Just as the therapist will work to show the patient how to recognize what is happening in his or her inner life and to devise strategies for dealing with it, so the supervisor aims to facilitate the therapist's becoming aware of these phenomena, internalizing the observing capacity, and devising therapeutic responses to the patient. The repetition of these experiences is a kind of working through that builds the evolving therapist's independent capacities, just as psychotherapy brings about change in a patient's psychic and neural structure.

The supervisor shares his or her own knowledge and experience base in assisting the supervisee to work with dreams, slips of the tongue, enactments inside and outside the treatment setting, and other clues to meanings of which the patient is not aware. While they may form hypotheses about these meanings, the task is to facilitate the patient's own associations and inner awareness so that the patient may come to his or her own sense of what these things are all about. The art of interpretation then is that of advancing a hypothesis as a trial balloon rather than as an authoritative truth that the patient is obliged to accept and believe. The supervisor advocates a view of a working partnership between the patient and the therapist in which the patient has to be the source of conviction about his or her mental life. As therapists grow in their abilities, they are better able to maintain that sense of partnership—for which the supervisory relationship serves as a model.

As transference and countertransference elements emerge, the supervisor helps the therapist identify and understand them. A sign of progression in the therapist's development is the growing ability to detect both transference in the patient and countertransference in oneself. One must steer a path between the Scylla of interpreting as transference everything that happens and the Charybdis of overlooking obvious manifestations—both in the patient and in oneself. A third person as an objective observer is generally likely to be helpful in discerning transference and countertransference phenomena, which is why supervision or consultation is valuable for the most experienced of therapists—and crucial if there is a disruption of the therapeutic process or any indication of unjustifiable boundary crossings or ethical violations. One must always bear in mind that supervision is a relationship in its own right, where issues from the therapy relationship may be unconsciously reflected. Many experienced psychoanalysts and psychotherapists engage in study groups that provide peer consultation about their cases.

Analogous to therapy, supervision in the long middle phase should see the therapist growing in sensitivity to psychodynamic issues, skill in handling them with the patient, and independent thought and action with a good sense of timing and adaptation to each patient's unique characteristics. Irresolvable countertransference reactions and repetitive errors in judgment may be cause for the supervisor to advise that the therapist seek psychoanalysis or psychodynamic psychotherapy to get to the heart of the matter. On rare occasions, the supervisor and a trainee who is not progressing after much effort may come to the conclusion that other kinds of professional activity may be more suitable.

The middle phase of a long-term psychodynamic psychotherapy may seem tedious and unrewarding to any therapist. Supervisors can help sort out when a treatment is really stuck, when there is resistance or a negative therapeutic reaction going on that may provide clues as to what is threatening to the patient, when there is a countertransference reaction that is obscuring the therapist's awareness of important issues in the therapy, or when the dyadic pair are simply in the long, repetitive process of working through important insights and their implications. At times, the supervisor may have to guide the therapist in confronting the patient about his or her failure to use insights to bring about significant changes in symptoms, behavior, or personality patterns. Sometimes the gratifications in the treatment process itself can be an impediment to change and have to be tactfully challenged. The psychoanalytic concept of negative therapeutic reaction[14, 15] may be useful in understanding an impasse in the treatment. Such impediments to further progress must be sorted out from a situation where the treatment has really accomplished its primary purpose and neither the patient nor the therapist has recognized that it is time to begin preparing for termination.

## TERMINATION

Inexperienced therapists may tend to underestimate the emotional importance to the patient of concluding their treatment. For many patients, termination is a significant loss that brings to mind other major losses in their lives. The supervisor needs to be assured that sufficient time and attention are devoted to the termination process of the treatment, to allow the patient to work through what this step means in the overall context of his or her relationships and emotional life. The longer and more intensive the psychodynamic psychotherapy has been, the longer the period usually will be between the decision to terminate and the final session. In any case, it is advisable for therapist and patient to discuss termination for more than one session before making a definite decision and setting a date. Beginning therapists should work closely with their supervisors during this phase.

Termination may present difficulties to the therapist as well. The treatment relationship is a form of attachment that works both ways. The therapist has generally come to like the patient and to be invested in the patient's ongoing tapestry of life, including relationships, creative work, freed-up potentialities, and personal victories and defeats. Not to be part of this anymore is hard for any therapist, seasoned or not. If one has a personal difficulty around separation, finds it hard to yield power or control of other people, or has an unusually gratifying investment in the patient, the supervisor or consultant may have to help the therapist work this through by self-analysis or taking it into a personal therapy. After the termination, the therapist may feel twinges of missing the patient, curiosity about what has subsequently occurred, or even grief. Supervisees can be helped to accept these feelings as expectable. Sometimes the patient and therapist may agree to have occasional follow-up visits, but the decision about this has to be made for the patient's welfare, not the therapist's, and consultation or supervision is valuable in considering it.

## PSYCHODYNAMIC PSYCHOTHERAPY AND OTHER MODALITIES OF TREATMENT

Just as many patients cannot be easily categorized by diagnosis because they present multiple symptom patterns (commonly called "comorbidity," as if multiple diseases were involved), so some patients may require a combination of therapeutic approaches. The patient may be best served by a *combination of medication and psychotherapy*—an evidence-based approach to more severely ill patients—or by combining elements commonly identified with multiple psychotherapeutic approaches. Psychodynamic issues can greatly affect *compliance with medications* and clinical assessment of their effects so that they may have to be addressed in the course of medication management. In regard to medication when both the supervisor and the therapist are psychiatrists, they will have to decide whether it is best for the supervisor to oversee the medication management as well as the psychotherapy. On the one hand, this may be more efficient, and it models a desired mode of the psychiatrist who can deal with both modalities in an integrated treatment. It also has the advantage of not dividing the possibilities for transference phenomena involving supervisors. On the other hand, the two modalities will compete for time in the supervision, and psychodynamic supervisors may not have expertise in medication management.

Therapeutic strategies commonly identified with *cognitive-behavioral therapy* have long been used in psychodynamic therapy, although they may be described in different terms. Freud[14] advised phobic patients to engage in something similar to what is now called systematic desensitization by incrementally attempting to encounter elements of the feared situation so that the underlying mental contents could be brought into the treatment without overwhelming the ego strength of the patient. Psychodynamic therapists have long confronted patients with observations of dysfunctional thought patterns such as catastrophizing or negation, usually looking beyond identifying the pattern to discern its defensive function. What psychodynamic therapists would see as the conscious tip of an unconscious iceberg of fantasy constructions that control emotional responses and behavior may be called automatic thoughts by cognitive-behavioral therapists; therapists of both persuasions would assist the patient to identify the thoughts, though the psychodynamic therapist would look further at the unconscious determinants. The advantage of future cognitive-behavioral therapists' learning of psychodynamic psychotherapy is that psychodynamic understanding may be useful in dealing with resistance or failure to follow the exercises of cognitive-behavioral therapy, even though the unconscious aspects would not be pursued.

*Interpersonal psychotherapy*, originally a simplified research version of psychodynamic therapy, addresses here-and-now aspects of grief and loss, major role changes, role confusions, and so on—all of which are familiar territory in psychodynamic therapy. *Supportive psychotherapy* can be enriched by psychodynamic understanding, though the role of transference and seeking insight would be managed differently, and issues around dependency in the therapy relationship might be more prominent. Again, techniques and concepts from the other therapeutic modality may be helpful in conducting the primary approach, although the supervisor should maintain clarity about what techniques are being used and their underlying rationale.

In all psychotherapies and in psychiatric management of patients, the therapeutic alliance is crucial, and responses by either patient or therapist that interfere with the progress of treatment must be addressed. All therapeutic interventions, no matter what their theoretical basis, have to be assessed in terms of how they affect the patient. In sum, supervisors can demonstrate that familiarity with psychodynamic approaches may be useful in any treatment situation.

## DIFFICULT PATIENTS, SPECIAL NEEDS

Some patients present unusually challenging problems due to the severity of their presenting symptoms or an underlying personality disorder. Hostile patients may be very threatening, requiring special measures to assure the safety of patient, staff, and other patients while still maintaining a working alliance with the patient. Seductive patients call for special attention to avoid boundary violations while still maintaining a congenial and empathic approach to the patient. Passive, highly narcissistic, and/or overintellectualizing patients may leave the therapist feeling bored, detached, and unable to engage the patient. He or she may also feel alone in carrying the burden of making a substantive therapy happen. Suspicious or distrusting patients may require great patience and steadiness in demonstrating the therapist's goodwill, good intentions, grounding in reality, and strong commitment to the patient's welfare. Borderline patients cause the therapist to feel drawn into heroic efforts to help in one session, only to be savagely rejected in the next session. Patients with out-of-control behavior who are actually inflicting damage on others raise issues about the therapist's obligations to report or to warn other people; it is likely that effective psychodynamic therapy will have to be conditioned on the behavior being brought under control so that its sources can be understood, even if some kind of reporting to government agencies or external restraint is mandated legally or clinically necessary. Patients with multiple medical problems, patients who have many caretakers, and chronically ill patients who arrive with a long list of previous therapists—each present special challenges. In all these instances, the supervisor is called on to bring special expertise in helping the supervised therapist deal with the situation at hand. Experience, theory, published reports about managing particular patients, and objective distance all help the supervisor respond with hoped-for wisdom, often with a touch of improvisation.

Perhaps the key element for the supervisor in responding to these difficult patients is to help the supervisee look beyond the provocative behavior to the suffering person within. If this can be achieved, it is much easier not to be provoked, to recoil or withdraw, to be seduced or retaliate, or to be overly excited, angry, or hurt. While the patient may initially feel threatened and resist such an effort to look beyond the behavior to its cause and to make contact with the person inside, in the long run it may lead to effective therapy. Supervision or consultation, even sought by experienced therapists (who may themselves be supervisors), may be valuable in keeping a steady hand on the tiller.

## TEACHING PSYCHODYNAMIC THERAPY TO PSYCHIATRIC RESIDENTS IN THE CURRENT ENVIRONMENT

Supervising psychiatric residents learning psychodynamic therapy has always been a challenge, but contemporary conditions make it more so. Many residents enter training expecting to learn a largely biological psychiatry. A growing proportion do not have a liberal arts background or come from cultures where psychotherapy is infrequent or devalued.

For example, a highly capable resident who had graduated from medical school in his native Middle Eastern country demonstrated great skill in clinically evaluating and managing general psychiatry patients. He was cordial and conscientious in the supervision. However, patient after patient quit after a session or two, and with the few he could keep, he demonstrated little sensitivity to the patient's emotional life and tended to deal with issues very superficially. In discussing his negative evaluation report to the training director, he said that he had no preparation for this work because in his country there was no practice of psychotherapy and it was actively devalued. He was clearly trying hard to grasp this new mode of thinking, but it was foreign to him. In further work together, we found that warm and caring doctor–patient relationships were customary in his native land and could be a starting point in feeling more comfortable with psychotherapy.

The curriculum is charged with covering many diverse subjects, and residents oscillate through a series of time-limited clinical rotations that do not admit of long-term relationships with patients. Insurance limitations or complete lack of third-party coverage for clinics have drastically reduced the number of patients available for experience with long-term psychodynamic psychotherapy. Competition from other psychotherapies that are short term, much more limited in scope, structured, and more amenable to randomized, controlled, double-blind trials of efficacy—hence considered evidence based—also limits access to patients. Negative attitudes of other faculty compound the problem. In addition, reimbursement incentives to practice high-volume medication management rather than start a practice that includes in-depth psychotherapy appeal to graduating residents who carry huge educational loans. As a result, access to psychiatrists who can offer full-service care with both medications and psychodynamic psychotherapy is becoming increasingly limited, and those who provide it are in demand.

The psychodynamic supervisor is thus challenged both to achieve sufficient clinical immersion with a resident to facilitate a meaningful developmental process as a therapist and to engage that resident in continuing a career path that includes psychodynamic psychotherapy or, for that matter, psychotherapy of any sort.

Fortunately, the power of psychodynamic psychotherapy does exert itself. In the first place, it helps patients in a way that demonstrates to the open-minded resident that this is a unique and powerful treatment that many patients need. Second, the intellectual stimulation of the psychodynamic approach appeals to residents as an enrichment of their lives and their approach to all patients. The depth and dynamism of psychoanalytic thought ensure its survival in spite of many opposing forces, as has always been the case. The biological revolution in psychiatry has now led to developments that bring together the elements of neurobiology, cognitive neuroscience, and psychoanalysis in a way that undermines the Cartesian dualism of mind and body.[16, 17] Psychoanalytic concepts of mental processes are found to parallel neurobiology in heuristically valuable ways. Finally, the supervisor him- or herself, as an example of someone who has conducted a richly satisfying, effective career in helping suffering people and made a decent living doing so, is a model that inspires residents to look beyond their immediate situation to a gratifying career that includes practicing psychodynamic psychotherapy.

## SUPERVISION OF PSYCHODYNAMIC PSYCHOTHERAPY IN OTHER MENTAL HEALTH PROFESSIONS

It is beyond the scope of this chapter or my direct experience to convey more than a few impressions gleaned from colleagues in other professions about the status of supervision of psychodynamic psychotherapy in psychology, social work, and clinical counseling. Graduate psychology training programs in the United States are divided into two types—Ph.D. programs offering training in both in-depth research and clinical practice and Psy.D. programs that present the scientific base but more greatly emphasize clinical practice. A survey of faculty preferences in graduate psychology programs showed that Ph.D. programs are dominated by a cognitive-behavioral orientation (65 percent of faculty), whereas in Psy.D. programs the faculty are about 30 percent psychodynamic/psychoanalytic, 30 percent cognitive-behavioral, 20 percent systems/family systems, and the remainder humanistic or behavioral in orientation.[18] Among graduate programs in both clinical psychology and social work, there is wide variation among programs in the degree of importance attached to the psychodynamic perspective, with certain well-known schools strongly identified with it but in the minority. There is a literature on enhancing the role and skills of supervision in both social work and clinical counseling, and psychodynamic issues appear to play a significant part in the discussion. For example, a paper in the counseling literature presents "five common supervision dilemmas": coping with shame and anxiety, understanding the parallel process, tolerating powerful affect in the client and the therapist, enhancing introspective curiosity, and providing support and confrontation.[19] Transference and countertransference figure heavily in approaching these dilemmas. Colleagues in the nonmedical fields echoed my own concern, as a psychiatrist, about the decline in prominence of a psychodynamic/psychoanalytic perspective while sensing a swing of the pendulum as the need for the distinctive insights of that perspective becomes apparent. This has been evident in the high interest shown in postgraduate psychotherapy courses offered by psychoanalytic institutes,[20] especially when they include a component of supervision.[21, 22]

## NOTES

1. American Psychoanalytic Association, *Principles and Standards of Ethics for Psychoanalysts* (New York: American Psychoanalytic Association, 2005). available at www.apsa.org/ethicscode.pdf.

2. Jacob Arlow, "The Supervisory Situation," *Journal of the American Psychoanalytic Association* 11 (1963): 576–94.

3. Stephen B. Bernstein, "Commentary," *Journal of the American Psychoanalytic Association* 48 (2000): 381–91.

4. American Psychiatric Association, *Resource Document: Documentation of Psychotherapy by Psychiatrists* (Arlington, Va.: American Psychiatric Association, 2002); available at www.psych.org/edu/other_res/lib_archives/archives/200202.pdf.

5. Jennifer L. Roberts, "Stage Fright in the Supervisory Process," in *The Supervisory Alliance*, ed. Susan Gill (Northvale, N.J.: Jason Aronson, 2001), 81–90.

6. Howard E. Gorman, "Interpreting Transference in Supervision," in Gill, *The Supervisory Alliance*, 181–99; originally published as "Interpreting Transference in the Supervision of Psychoanalytic Psychotherapy," *American Journal of Psychotherapy* 53 (2000): 452–66.

7. Marcia K. Goin and Frank Kline, "Countertransference: A Neglected Subject in Clinical Supervision," *American Journal of Psychiatry* 133 (1976): 41–44.

8. Winslow Hunt, "The Use of the Countertransference in Supervision," in Gill, *The Supervisory Alliance*, 165–79; originally published as "The Use of Countertransference in Supervision," *Journal of the American Academy of Psychoanalysis* 9 (1981): 361–73.

9. Paul A. Dewald, "Aspects of the Supervisory Process," *Annual of Psychoanalysis* 9 (1981): 75–89.

10. Susan Reifer, "Dealing with the Anxiety of Beginning Therapists in Supervision," in Gill, *The Supervisory Alliance*, 67–74.

11. Susan Gill, "Narcissistic Vulnerability in Supervisees: Ego Ideals, Self-Exposure, and Narcissistic Character Defenses," in *The Supervisory Alliance*, 19–34; originally published as "Narcissistic Vulnerability in Psychoanalytic Psychotherapy Supervisees: Ego Ideals, Self-Exposure and Narcissistic Character Defenses," *International Forum of Psychoanalysis* 8 (1999): 1–6.

12. Sydney Arkowitz, "Perfectionism in the Supervisee," in Gill, *The Supervisory Alliance*, 35–66; originally published in *Psychoanalysis and Psychotherapy* 8 (1990): 51–68.

13. Iris Levy, "Superego Issues in Supervision," in Gill, *The Supervisory Alliance*, 91–106.

14. Sigmund Freud, "Lines of Advance in Psycho-Analytic Therapy," in *The Standard Edition of the Complete Psychological Works of Sigmund Freud*, vol. 17, ed. James Strachey (London: International Universities Press, 1955), 157–68.

15. Joseph Sandler, Christopher Dare, and Alex Holder, "The Negative Therapeutic Reaction," in *The Patient and the Analyst* (New York: International Universities Press, 1992), 121–32.

16. Eric Kandel, "A New Intellectual Framework for Psychiatry," *American Journal of Psychiatry* 155 (1998): 457–69.

17. Eric Kandel, "Biology and the Future of Psychoanalysis: A New Intellectual Framework for Psychiatry Revisited," *American Journal of Psychiatry* 156 (1999): 505–24.

18. John C. Norcross, Patricia H. Castle, Michael A. Sayette, and Tracy J. Mayne, "The Psy.D.: Heterogeneity in Practitioner Training," *Professional Psychology: Research and Practice* 35 (2004): 412–19.

19. Carl F. Rak and Paula J. Britton, "Common Counselor Struggles with Supervision," *Journal for the Professional Counselor* 12 (1997): 55–65.

20. Robert S. White and Caryle Perlman, "Spotlight on Psychotherapy Training Programs," *The American Psychoanalyst*, 37, no. 4 (2003): 13 (introduces "Special Section: Psychotherapy Training," 13–17, with reports on programs in Cleveland, Boston, and Chicago; available at www.apsa.org/tap/vol37no5.pdf).

21. Richard Lightbody, "New Life for Cleveland's Psychotherapy Program," *The American Psychoanalyst* 37, no. 4 (2003): 14, 17.

22. Thomas H. Ogden, "On Psychoanalytic Supervision," *International Journal of Psychoanalysis* 86 (2005): 1265–80.

# 4

# Discussing the Undiscussable: The Limits of Supervision

*Francis T. Varghese*

In one of his earliest observations on the phenomena of transference, Freud noted that the analysand would make reference directly or obscurely to some peculiarity or distinctive characteristic in the analyst. That this is so should not be surprising. Although the notion that the psychodynamically orientated therapist is opaque and anonymous to the patient is a myth, it nevertheless is the case that therapists are usually parsimonious in revealing information about themselves. This is so as not to interfere with the development of the transference and impede the therapeutic process but also to protect themselves and set the boundaries of the therapeutic frame.

In every psychotherapeutic encounter, the patient is seeking to develop a relationship with a therapist. As therapy progresses, we get to know the patient more and more to an extent that perhaps nobody else has known him. The patient is also seeking to get to know the therapist but is thwarted by the limited information the therapist provides. In fact, however, there is much we reveal about ourselves unknowingly to a curious patient who can make judgments or guesses about our background and personalities from the pictures on our walls, the nature of our furniture, the tidiness or untidiness of our desks, the books displayed, photographs on the desk, and even the clothes we wear and how we wear them. In the thirst for knowledge about the therapist, the patient will also rely on gesture, tone of voice, or turn of phrase, which we may not be ourselves aware of, in order to form judgments. Attention will also be paid to our affective response to what is said in therapy and also our sense of humor. Thus, as therapists, we are being observed as well as observing. Indeed, the more opaque we tend to be, the more likely it is that the patient will rely on subtle observations. The patient may or may not be accurate about the conclusions made, based on appearance or detection of attitude or reaction. However, whatever the case, the issue is likely to be played out in the transference, and therapists need to be aware about this. The task of the supervisor is how to discuss these issues that are matters we do not generally want to talk about without crossing the boundary from supervision to therapy.

It is becoming increasingly accepted that the form the transference takes is determined as much by factors in the patient's past and the present state of his object relationships as by the events in therapy, including the behavior and feelings of the therapist. Thus, transference is now seen as the creation of both parties in the therapeutic space.[1] It follows then that the person of the therapist, including his "peculiarities" and his beliefs, feelings, and attitudes, must influence how the transference manifests. If this is the case, then therapists need to be aware of their peculiarities or vulnerabilities and to have an understanding of how these matters may impact on a patient in therapy. Discomfort about such aspects or lack of acceptance of them has the potential to impede the process of therapy and to create blocks in the empathic relationship between therapist and patient.

One of the tasks of psychodynamic psychotherapy supervision is to facilitate in the supervisees the capacity to see how any peculiarities they have—any particular characteristic of their person and their beliefs and feelings—can influence the therapeutic relationship. The supervisor, however, ought not to cross the line into being the supervisee's therapist, but, in discussing the personal in a supervisee who may be reluctant to examine the personal or seek to deny peculiarities or their significance, it may be difficult to know where the line is between supervision and therapy.

It is one thing to invite supervisees to reflect on their feelings at a particular moment in therapy or in response to the patient's statements or behavior, or to reflect on how their words or actions may have influenced a patient's behavior. Such challenges can be dealt with by intellectualization or even obfuscation and pretended insight, and a supervisor is unlikely to be confronting on such issues beyond a certain point. It is an entirely different matter to inquire of supervisees as to how they believed their skin color might be impacting on the patient being discussed or whether a seemingly obscure statement by the patient could indicate a reference to an obvious physical disability in the therapist or issues of sexual orientation. In such a situation, the supervisee is confronted with what may be an unstated core issue for him, and the supervisor's inquiry may be perceived as an attack on the core self and one's sense of being and, moreover, as an intrusion outside the supervision frame, which sometimes it is.

Therapists in training—for that matter all therapists—present several personae and "identities" that could be regarded as "false selves" to their patients. This identity or identities, the "I" in William James's formulation of the duality of self,[2] prevents or protects the core self or true self (the "me") from appearing. While as therapists we become increasingly comfortable with the patient's transferences focusing on aspects of our "identity" to the extent that we are a necessary "fantasy figure" for the patient, we are uncomfortable when the transference touches a core aspect of ourselves that we do not wish the patient to be aware of or even to notice. But there are certain aspects of the "me" that we cannot easily disguise or hide. These include our bodily structure, physiognomy, skin color, and indeed any aspect of our outward appearance, such as accent or even our weight.

The core self or "me" has several aspects and is also private. We share aspects with special others only in intimate moments, but to the extent that one's body or body image is part of the core self, this aspect is necessarily visible. If the core self is healthy, we tend to be comfortable about our bodies and how we look to others, but there may nevertheless be aspects we dislike or are uncomfortable with. Whether we are comfortable with these aspects or not, on the whole this is an area we do not like to talk about in supervision for fear of inadvertently causing offense, or because of the dictates of so-called political correctness or because the supervisor has difficulties in dealing with these issues.

The following case histories illustrate the importance of addressing issues that supervisors and therapists very often are unwilling to address. In these cases, which have been rendered unidentifiable, the discussion concerns psychiatric residents, but the principles apply equally to other mental health professionals.

## BODILY PECULIARITIES

A male psychiatric resident suffered a significant neurological event during medical school training. He recovered almost fully but was left with a residual mild facial nerve weakness. Although mild, the palsy was obvious, but the neurological condition was in no way impairing. In presenting to his supervisor a prospective case of a young woman who had been referred for psychotherapy, he was of the opinion, after having seen the patient on three different occasions, that she was probably not a suitable candidate for psychodynamic psychotherapy. This puzzled the supervisor, as there was little information the candidate presented that sounded like an impediment to psychotherapy, and, moreover, the data presented suggested that, far from being an unsuitable candidate for psychotherapy, the patient was a good candidate.

On exploring the issue further, the resident stated that he did not find the patient "likable" and that he had read somewhere that this was important for psychotherapy to be successful. However, he could provide no reason why the patient should be unlikable other than that he found her manner irritating and, adding as an afterthought, that she was "intrusive." When the nature of the patient's intrusiveness was explored, the resident reluctantly revealed that the patient had stated when discussing her relationship with her father that he had suffered some sort of stroke when she was in her teenage years, leaving him with a significant neurological impediment. The patient revealed that her father was very sensitive about his impediment and that for her own part she felt very guilty that she was embarrassed by him in the presence of her friends. It was only as she grew older that she realized how awful it must have been for him to have the impediment and be aware of her embarrassment, adding, "You must know what it must have been like, doctor." On discussion of the issues, the resident was able to see that his "dislike" of the patient and her intrusiveness was a reflection of his sensitivity about his slight cosmetic defect and the patient touching on this area.

The resident was then able to appreciate how a physical "defect" in him had facilitated a very rapid development of a transference-countertransference relationship in the therapeutic space created by their interaction together. It turned out that the patient was an excellent candidate for psychotherapy, and the resident went on to continue this with her.

In this case, the neurological incident can be seen not only to have damaged the resident's nervous system but also to have affected his self-image and body image, not just what he displayed to the external world, which was relatively trivial, but also his internalized view of himself. He had been congratulated and, indeed, had congratulated himself on his recovery and overcoming disability to the extent of being able to complete his medical training and enter specialist training and form a long-term conjugal relationship, yet he carried a sense of personal defect. In his encounter with his patient, he was able to learn that his defect was no more than a peculiarity and, far from interfering with his relationship, the patient had enhanced it.

A female supervisee was engaged in the treatment of a female patient with anorexia nervosa and borderline personality disorder. The supervisee had a significant problem with being overweight, a matter about which she was quite sensitive. In supervision, it was clear that she was having serious problems with a very difficult patient. She described feeling helpless and felt she was the subject of unreasonable attacks on her by her patient. She was troubled by her feelings of anger toward the patient and her wishes that the patient would not turn up for psychotherapy sessions or drop out altogether.

There were long periods of time during therapy when the patient would say nothing and any attempt to engage her was greeted by flippant remarks.

Moreover, the patient would frequently criticize the supervisee for lacking understanding and rejected any attempts to help her understand her feelings. She claimed that the supervisee did not like her and preferred other patients and that she would get very angry if she forgot something she had said from several sessions before.

In one session, the patient, in discussing her relationship with her mother, described her as a "fat, lazy slob" who only had time for herself and was preoccupied with her own needs. Her greatest fear was that she would become like her mother, and she had vowed to strive to be different. Despite her hostility toward her mother, she remained dependent and visited her on a weekly basis, only to feel worn out and distressed at the end of the visits. "She just sits there while I am expected to run around her and do everything."

In this case it seemed clear to the supervisor that the patient's transference rage was being played out in the language of weight, and it was hardly surprising that the therapist would feel under attack. Clearly the supervisee needed assistance in dealing with a very difficult patient. She felt overwhelmed by the patient and felt an urge to counterattack, which had the potential to have significant negative consequences for the patient with a risk of self-harm. The supervisor was reluctant to discuss the issue of weight directly. Rather, there was a general discussion on the origins of hate in the transference in terms of object relations theory and how this might be handled in therapy so as to repair the disjunction in the therapeutic relationship. The supervisee was also encouraged to examine her own feelings of countertransference hate and what this might mean in understanding projective identification. The supervisee did not feel helped by the supervisor's insights, ending the supervision session with "but I still don't know what to do."

The therapy continued in much the same manner as previously with the therapist feeling increasingly frustrated and angry in her attempts to contain the patient's rage and destructive impulses. She was able to understand both empathically and theoretically how the patient's rage was not really directed toward her but rather was a function of the patient's pathological relationship with her mother. But any attempt to feed back to the patient her empathic understanding of the patient's situation was met by dismissive statements, such as "How would you know?" or "I know how I feel" . . . "what are you doing to help me?" . . . "do something about it." Any attempt at interpretation was also rejected. "I know my mother was a cold and unfeeling person, but why can't you be different?"

The therapy continued for several sessions until the supervisee reported that there had been a major change in the patient's demeanor. When the content of the therapeutic session was examined, rather sheepishly she revealed that she brought up the issue of her own weight problems with the patient, adding, "I know you are not supposed to do this." In the session concerned, the patient had again proceeded to berate her mother and then proceeded to berate the therapist for being unhelpful and unfeeling. The supervisee said, "I just blurted out" . . . "I now realize that you are angry with me, not because you feel I'm like your mother but because I am overweight like your mother." The patient was quite taken aback by the statement. She proceeded to defend herself by saying that she would never be so cruel as to make references to any person's weight or, indeed, attack people on the basis of their weight. The patient then became tearful and described how as a child she was embarrassed by her mother's overweight and, moreover, how she was teased as a child for being overweight herself. She went on to describe how horrible she felt as a child and how she hated her body and, with it, herself. She went on to say, "I know doctors aren't allowed to talk about their feelings" . . . "I realize you must know a little bit of how it was like for me, and I realize that I must have hurt you by always talking about my mother's obesity." The therapist did not reveal anything more about herself and at this point told the patient that an apology was not required. What was more important was that she understood how her feelings about her mother and her relationship with her mother were affecting what was going on in her therapy.

In considering this case, it is not being argued that the supervisee's overweight was necessarily the critical issue between the patient and therapist. It is likely that the patient's feelings about her mother would have emerged in any case with another therapist of normal weight, although it may have taken a different form. Neither is it being argued that the therapist's weight was somehow or the other a "block" to therapy and that addressing the issue was essential in therapy progressing. Clearly there would have to be several ways of dealing with the therapeutic impasse and the patient's negative transference other than a self-referential statement about the therapist's weight. What the case illustrates is a reluctance of all parties—the patient, the therapist, and the supervisor—to state the obvious and how a statement of the obvious can sometimes lead to a way out of a therapeutic impasse.

For the supervisor's part, his reluctance to discuss what seemed obvious is understandable. He is in a particular relationship with the supervisee, which limits the extent to which he can intrude in a personal area, especially if there is likely to be sensitivity about the particular aspect. The supervisor's reliance on theoretical formulations of what was going on was not found to be particularly helpful even though the theoretical formulations were essentially correct.

Could the supervisor have acted differently to benefit the therapist's treatment of the patient? It would have been a very insensitive supervisor who asked her, "Do you think the patient is in some way referring to your own weight problem?" or "How do you think your own overweight is affecting the transference?" However, the issue could have been addressed sensitively earlier in the assessment of the patient for psychotherapy. The choice of patient ought to have been discussed then, including what the supervisee's feelings were about individuals with eating disorders. It seems likely that a reasonably self-reflective person training in psychotherapy, when confronted with a question as to why a particular patient is being selected for psychotherapy or what their attitudes might be to patients with eating disorders, would have drawn attention to their own difficulties with weight. The supervisor could then have prepared her as to how these issues might emerge in therapy. An important task for a supervisor is to ensure that each supervisee reflects on whether there is anything about him- or herself that have made them select a particular patient to help through psychotherapy.

## SEXUAL ORIENTATION

A male supervisee from a conservative religious background was treating a young man with narcissistic issues. A significant difficulty for the patient was the instability of his relationships, although he seemed to have no difficulty attracting a string of women who indulged him both emotionally and sexually. The supervisee did not seem to have any major difficulties in dealing with the patient's behavior as reported even though it clashed with his own values. In supervision, he was able to discuss the clash of values and also his occasional envy of the patient. He seemed sensitive to the patient's idealizing transference and his own countertransference reactions.

During one supervision session, he mentioned, almost in passing, that he wondered whether the patient would be better off with a female therapist. In exploring this issue, he could not provide any coherent reason why the gender of the therapist should be of importance. The supervisor suspected that the young supervisee's problems leading him to consider a change of therapist might have been related to his own attraction to the patient and unacknowledged homosexual impulses. However, the supervisor was reluctant to suggest this or address the issue in any way. In the first place, the supervisor was aware of the resident's religious views and was concerned about the extent to which any exploration of this area might be too confronting. Moreover, the supervisor had to be aware of the boundary between supervision and engaging in what may seem to be therapy on a very sensitive issue. The supervisor opted rather to discuss in general terms the nature of countertransference phenomena and their relationship to transference and to the importance of exploring these issues, including when therapists have unusual ideas about the patient during the therapy or after it.

At the next session, the supervisee, in discussing the progress of psychotherapy, stated that the patient had revealed that for many years he had been concerned about his sexuality and whether he was homosexual. He even offered the opinion that his promiscuity with women may be an attempt to cover up his hidden homosexuality. In discussing the details of the session as it unfolded, it was clear that the supervisee had handled the patient's conflict over sexual orientation quite well and empathetically. He was also able to discuss with the supervisor his attitudes to homosexuality, indicating that despite his religious convictions, he had no prejudice toward homosexuals. Without any assistance from the supervisor, the supervisee was able to now understand that his previous statement that the patient may be better off with a female therapist was a reaction to his own, then unconscious, homosexual impulses that emerged during the treatment of the patient. To the supervisor's embarrassment, he gently chided the supervisor for obfuscating on the issue in the previous session. "It was so obvious, you must have known." The supervisor was then able to acknowledge that the previous supervision session may have been more useful if the supervisor had not made assumptions about his attitude to homosexuality in light of his religious affiliation.

Issues of gender and sexual orientation are essential to an individual's identity and core self. This is a difficult area to discuss openly, even in a therapeutic situation, let alone in a supervisory situation. Moreover, deep exploration of these issues is inappropriate and may be harmful within supervision.

In this case, the supervisor made assumptions about the supervisee's difficulties and prejudices that were incorrect. These were, to some extent, a reflection of the supervisor's own difficulties and prejudices. Both learned from a situation where what was forbidden to be talked about could be discussed.

Despite decreasing prejudice and general acceptance of homosexuality, the supervision of therapists who are treating a homosexual patient remains a difficult task for complex reasons. Inexperienced therapists are often drawn into offering psychotherapy to a patient of a different sexual orientation without considering the potential difficulties or, indeed, their own motivations and unstated aims for therapy. Therapists need to explore what aspects of the patient they wish to change and why and whether this is what the patient wants. Moreover, the therapist may have ideas of normality with respect to relationships and lifestyle that may not be "normal" within the patient's peer group, culture, or preferred lifestyle. The therapist may claim no prejudice against homosexuality and no wish to change the sexual orientation but nevertheless may highly value long-term conjugal relationships. This may not be what the patient or his group values or, indeed, what the patient seeks or considers to be healthy. Sometimes therapists opt for treatment of a homosexual individual as a way of dealing with their own conflicts about sexual orientation. If this is the motivation, it is unlikely to be helpful to the patient and may be harmful to both. Understandably, it is one of the most sensitive issues to discuss in supervision and all the more difficult because of the constraints of supervision as against therapy. However, failure to explore—and sometimes to confront—may be harmful to the patient whose treatment is being supervised.

In a teaching presentation for a group of residents, a case of a seventeen-year-old male student was presented. The presenting problem was that his parents were concerned that, unlike his friends of a similar age, he does not have a girlfriend and shows little interest in asking any girl out for a date. His parents are concerned that he could be homosexual and wonder if anything can be done about it. For his part, the young man states that he has always been very shy with girls and in any case is not ready for relationships. He states that he has wondered about his sexuality and does not believe that he is homosexual. He also states that if he were homosexual, he would wish that this were not the case.

The subsequent discussion of the clinical issues by the residents is dominated by the debate between those who argue that the therapeutic focus should be on getting the young man to accept his homosexuality and even that he be encouraged to meet other homosexuals and those who argue that the therapeutic endeavor should be focused on dealing with his shyness toward girls, including education about sexuality and social skills training. The debate is essentially a politicization of the clinical situation according to the beliefs and prejudices of the residents toward homosexuality. Meanwhile, the patient's individual needs and an exploration of the totality of his situation are in danger of being obscured by an ideological agenda centered around sexual orientation. The supervisor in such a situation needs to be able to bring the focus back to the needs of the individual by pointing out how judgments about direction of therapy are affected by prejudice as well as one's sexual orientation.

## RACE AND ETHNICITY

A therapist of South Asian origin sought supervision for the treatment of a patient he has been seeing for three months, as circumstances necessitated a change in supervisor. The patient was a young professional woman who came to therapy following distress at the breakup of a relationship. The supervisor inquired of him as to how his ethnic origins had impacted on the psychotherapy to date. He was quite taken aback by the directness of the question and replied that he did not think it had had any effect. He considered that there had been a good therapeutic alliance. He believed that the patient had made progress and that transference issues had been entirely positive, reflecting her need to have a sympathetic and understanding parental figure in distinction to her hypercritical mother and absent father. The patient, moreover, had not made any inquiries as to his ethnic origins or commented on it in therapy to date.

The supervisor pointed out that the supervisee's ethnic origin was probably his most distinctive feature to the patient. She knew nothing else about him other than his name and that he was a doctor. Consequently, it would be most unlikely that his physical appearance did not have some impact on the therapeutic relationship and, indeed, the manifestations of transference. He discounted that this could be true, stating that he was comfortable with his ethnic origins. He said that he had never encountered prejudice in his training or work as a doctor, and the only patients who had referred to his ethnic origin did so when they were psychotic.

It then emerged that for the first fifteen minutes of the most recent session, the patient had talked about her distress and anger about prejudice toward people of Islamic origin since terrorist attacks internationally. She believed that the present politicians were ignorant about Muslims and that, if only they knew them better, they would be less alarmed. When asked if he considered that this was in some way a statement about his ethnic origins or whether the patient was seeking to discuss his ethnic origins, he was skeptical. He stated that while he shared the patient's views, he would never discuss his personal views. Moreover, the patient would not have known he was Muslim or belonged to some other faith, as he had never discussed religion. When asked how he would have responded if the patient had, instead of defending the rights of Muslims, made derogatory statements about them in light of what was being said publicly in the press, he replied that it would be inappropriate to discuss political issues with a patient. He agreed that such a situation may make it difficult for him to treat the patient and stated that this was not necessarily a true countertransference issue but a "reality issue."

Later in the same therapy session, the patient had gone on to talk about her mother. She considered that her own mother's problems had arisen from the fact that her grandparents were from different cultures in that her grandmother was Irish-Australian while her grandfather was a Greek immigrant. She stated that her grandfather did not understand Australian ways and that there was conflict as to what was appropriate behavior. Moreover, her mother considered that her father did not understand her because he came from a foreign culture. For her part, the patient found her grandfather to be cold and distant. She would have liked to have known him better, but he was undemonstrative and would not reveal much about himself. On the other hand, she curiously identified with her grandmother, whom she considered was adventurous in marrying a man from a different ethnic background despite her parents' concerns. She added that from her own experience she could understand why her grandmother would prefer somebody who was not Australian. She went on to describe her negative experiences with men.

It seemed to the supervisor that complex transference dynamics were occurring against a background of ethnicity and culture. It is possible that her defense of Muslims was an expression of her positive transference and a wish to seek an alliance and connectedness with the therapist. Alternatively, it could have been explored as a reaction formation to her aggressive impulses toward her therapist. Her comments about the grandfather's cultural difference impacting on his understanding of her mother could be understood as her reflection of her doubts about the therapist's capacity to understand her. Furthermore, her comments about her identification with her grandmother could have indicated that there was an erotic element in the transference. When these issues were discussed, the supervisee found it difficult to accept that the references may have been in any way oblique references to him as a therapist and the ethnic difference. He was skeptical that he could have such an impact on the patient. He also professed some skepticism as to the concept of transference. He stated that his approach was supportive and cognitive in helping the patient adjust to her new circumstances, although he could accept that he was a parental figure for his patient.

However, as therapy progressed, he began to pay particular attention to the patient's references to ethnicity and culture, which were sometimes oblique. He then was able to see more clearly the development, nuances, and vicissitudes of the transference and the relationship of this to his own feelings and actions. Moreover, in going through his notes of the previous sessions, he was able to identify allusions to ethnic difference and cultural issues even early in the therapy. The patient had referred to books she had read and how a certain book by an Indian author had taught her a lot about Indian culture. She referred to her own minority status as one-quarter Greek. She had read a book on how Alexander the Great was an important influence in Indian history. She also described how she had experimented with making a curry. Most of her references were positive. However, she also mentioned that Indian and Pakistani cricketers had been found to be engaged in bribery and that the Australian cricket team had unfair decisions against them by the umpires in India. She also made reference to whether people from different cultures could understand each other. By now paying attention to the references to ethnicity, he was able to see how the transference was focused on a particular aspect of himself. He then began to understand his own feelings and how they were in turn influenced by his culture and value system.

In increasingly multicultural, multiethnic, and multiracial societies, psychotherapeutic encounters will take place across cultural, ethnic, and racial boundaries. In most cases, this is unlikely to be problematic and may indeed enhance the richness of the psychotherapeutic experience. Nevertheless, therapists need to be aware of how the differences may manifest in the therapeutic relationship in subtle, unacknowledged ways. Moreover, supervisors need to be not only cognizant of these issues but also willing to raise them in the supervision process. For various reasons, supervisors are sometimes unwilling to do so, and, in addition, therapists may also be unwilling to discuss these issues with supervisors.

The term "pretransference" has been used to describe a patient's feelings toward a therapist of a different ethnic or racial background even before any therapy has commenced. This refers to a set of feelings, attitudes, prejudices, or identifications that a patient may have toward the therapist based on the therapist's ethnic origins.[3] It is inevitable that the subsequent therapeutic relationship will be shaped to some extent by the pretransference. Therapists need to be aware of this so that it can be sensitively addressed if required. It follows then that supervisors also need to be able to talk about these issues with their supervisees. This may be difficult if there are taboos, including institutional taboos, to discussing these matters.

In societies where the relationship between ethnic or racial groups is governed by unstated and culturally determined but nevertheless powerful rules and even taboos, the problem of psychotherapy across ethnic and racial divide is compounded. For instance, if the culture does not accept, or there is significant negativity toward, sexual relationships across a racial or ethnic divide, then it is extremely difficult to address transference issues, whether or not there is an erotic element. Such a situation may be extremely challenging for a supervisor. This can be particularly so if the supervision itself is across an ethnic or a racial divide, where the supervisor's own issues with respect to ethnic relationships and behavior may be an issue.

## CONCLUSIONS

Training a clinician in the science and art of psychotherapy is arguably one of the more difficult educational tasks. While theory can be learned by traditional methods, the application of this can be taught only by experience. This experience must be supervised by a clinician who has skills and experience in psychotherapy. Many trainees in psychotherapy expect that the supervisor will be able to tell them what to say and do in a particular situation. Instead, the most important task is to learn how to listen, including listening to what is going on within oneself during psychotherapy. It is a big step when the supervisee understands that this is what it is about, not just the application of a particular technique. Supervisors need to provide an environment and a supervisory frame where supervisees can be open about themselves and, in particular, what goes on within them during therapy without the risk of the supervision becoming something more akin to therapy. The supervisor must be not only aware of the limits of supervision but also prepared to set limits.

The accounts given in this chapter, which provide snippets of the supervision process, illustrate what may happen when what obviously needs to be talked about is sometimes avoided because of potential sensitivity. It is hoped that they also illustrate how talking about the obvious, whether with the assistance of the supervisor or not, can enhance the psychotherapeutic process and the supervisory experience.

## NOTES

1. Glen O. Gabbard, "Countertransferences: The Emerging Common Ground," *International Journal of Psychoanalysis* 76 (1995): 475–88.
2. Russell Meares, *Intimacy and Alienation: Memory, Trauma and Personal Being* (London: Routledge, 2000).
3. Frank T. Varghese, "The Effect of Racial Difference on the Therapeutic Relationship in Individual Psychotherapy," *Australian and New Zealand Journal of Psychiatry* 17 (1983): 329–33.

# 5

# Improving Supervisory Skills: An Exercise in Lifelong Learning

*Marcia Kraft Goin*

One of the most important educational functions that clinicians perform is supervision of the clinical work of trainees and other mental health professionals. Yet they usually take on this task with no particular training to define or hone their educational skills. Supervision of another clinician's psychotherapy, like psychotherapy itself, usually takes place privately without others watching the supervisory process. Consequently, educators commonly develop their individual or even egocentric manner of supervision on their own. Reading the literature and adopting techniques recalled from one's own supervision are some of the means they may use. However, there should be more directly relevant information and educational opportunities available for those who take on this significant challenge. Conferences organized to directly address strategies for supervision, small- and large-group discussions for those who work in this area, and looking at videotapes of highly valued supervisors are some of the methods we have found useful in working with those who teach in a psychiatric residency training program. These are of equal value to all mental health professionals, including those who are in clinical practice.

In the late 1990s, the American Psychiatric Association's Committee on Psychotherapy organized an educational program, Advanced Strategies for Teaching Psychotherapy, as a one-day meeting prior to the regularly scheduled meeting of the American Association of Directors of Residency Training. We wondered, Would anyone come? Attending meant extra expense and required residency training directors to spend another day away from their regularly scheduled work. To our surprise and delight, more than one hundred signed up for the meeting. At the end of the day, after hearing effective examples presented by experts in psychodynamic, cognitive, and interpersonal therapy, they were eager for more. Educating the educators seemed like not only a necessary but also a much-desired function. Many expressed their appreciation that a conference such as this had been scheduled, as it filled a major void in their postgraduate education. First, they had been trainees with supervision provided; then, usually without any specialized training in education, they were suddenly supervising the clinical work of others. The conference helped fill that void. The attendees planned to take the information back home to their clinical settings and institute continuing education in this area for others.

## WHAT DO SUPERVISEES VALUE?

Years ago, a colleague (Frank Kline) and I undertook to discover some of the qualities that make one an "outstanding supervisor." The category of "outstanding" was identified by the psychiatric residents' annual evaluation of their supervisors where they were asked on a confidential form to classify their supervisor as "outstanding," "very good," "good," or "poor." Their trainees evaluated some supervisors year after year as "outstanding," while others were more consistently considered to be "very good" or simply "good." We had our own hypotheses about the magic ingredient. Dr. Kline believed it to be something as unteachable as "charisma," and I thought we would find that these outstanding supervisors focused primarily on technique, that is, the "how to" of psychotherapy. We were both wrong.

In search of the answer, we videotaped twenty-four supervisors while they met with their trainees. Three supervisory sessions were videotaped for each supervisor, and they and their trainees identified the session that was most similar to the regular sessions that took place before the intrusion of a video camera. Not surprisingly, the third meeting was usually chosen as the most similar to regular supervision.

Dr. Kline and I then had the marvelously voyeuristic experience of looking at these tapes and doing a content analysis of each of the supervisors' interventions. What we learned, after all the analyses were complete, would not surprise any student of education. The valued supervisors were active teachers. They were active and focused and addressed their activity to the task at hand: the treatment of the patient under discussion. Some supervisors focused more on technique, or countertransference, or case formulation, but all were actively involved in the process. They were interested in the patient as well as the supervisee. They pushed the supervisee to conceptualize the problems and helped them reformulate the process in a useful way. By first forming a good working relationship with the supervisee, they could use this as a basis for assertive education.[1]

Dividing the supervisors into two groups with an equal distribution as to their ratings, we invited half of the twenty-four supervisors to attend two evening sessions devoted to talking about supervision. During those two evenings, they looked at and discussed edited sections from the supervision sessions of three of the "outstandingly" rated supervisors. We encouraged the attendees to think about what the observed supervisors did that trainees would find beneficial. We discouraged talk about negative qualities, consistently refocusing on the question, What is valuable? They could see that the educators were actively engaged with the residents in exploring the process of the patients' treatment, encouraging the supervisees to formulate hypotheses about that process, and providing suggestions about possible interventions. Not only did the supervisors enjoy the opportunity to talk about supervision, but in the ensuing year their evaluations improved as well. These supervisors evidenced greater activity in the supervision sessions that was directed at understanding the patient clinician treatment process and suggesting potentially useful interventions. Evaluations for those in the control group did not change. The good dinner and wine may have helped make the evening a pleasure and foster the 100 percent return for the second night, but it was obviously the educational experience that changed their behavior with their trainees.[2, 3]

## TODAY'S EDUCATIONAL CHALLENGES

The previously mentioned studies took place in the late 1960s. Unlike the mid-twentieth century, the twenty-first century is accompanied with a plethora of psychopharmacologic knowledge, exciting advances in neuroscience and gene structure, as well as an academic curriculum chock-full of the needed fundamentals for diagnosis and, in psychiatry, psychopharmacologic treatment. This leaves much less time for a leisurely exploration and understanding of intrapsychic phenomena and the finer elements of psychodynamic psychotherapy.

Along with this mix of expanding knowledge and limited time, we must also take into account the reality of today's depleted mental health care system. Most psychiatric residency training programs and other mental health professional training occurs at academic sites where there is limited ability to hospitalize and little time to talk with patients over an extended period of time. Public psychiatric facilities usually restrict their funds to the treatment of the severely mentally ill. This reflects not a prejudice against nonpsychotic patients but rather an attempt to deal with the realities of financial cutbacks. Thus, the psychotherapy educator often needs to use the clinical material presented by relatively ill patients to teach the fundamentals of the various psychotherapies. Enter the trainee: eager to learn, excited about the field, presented with volumes of data, and with limited time and resources. If ever there was a time when supervisors needed to be active and focused, this is it.

In the past few years, for example, the Residency Review Committee of the American College of Graduate Medical Education has recognized that psychotherapy education might be slipping away. This has led to the requirement that psychiatric residency programs certify their residents as competent by graduation in five psychotherapies: psychodynamic psychotherapy, cognitive psychotherapy, supportive psychotherapy, brief psychotherapy, and combined psychotherapy and psychopharmacology. Various objectives have been written describing what is meant by "competent." They can seem daunting when first read. However, having supervisors meet together and work through a thoughtful assessment of what is needed to achieve these competency objectives can serve to facilitate both a focus and a direction for the process of supervision. In addition, although these have been specifically written as directions for psychiatric residency training programs, they reflect core principles that are part of the work of all mental health professionals. Thus, they are a useful resource for all who supervise clinicians.

## CORE COMPETENCY REQUIREMENTS

To illustrate, consider the core competency expectations for psychodynamic psychotherapy. Andrews and Burruss, in their book *Core Competencies for Psychiatric Education: Defining, Teaching and Assessing Resident Competence*,[4] provide a list of expectations by which to judge if a psychiatric resident is "competent." These include the following:

1. Ability to recognize central dynamic issues
2. Ability to conceptualize a psychodynamic formulation
3. Ability to link understanding of the patient's past, present, and transference patterns to thoughts, feelings, and behaviors
4. Ability to describe the patient's major defensive organization
5. Ability to clarify, confront, and make interpretations at appropriate times. (108)

This list is direct and to the point. As a supervisor, I would agree with this list of expectations. I assume that if a group of supervisors spent a number of hours together brainstorming about what the outcome of their supervision should be, they would eventually come up with a list something like this. Probably it would be much longer, reflecting each clinician's special area of concern. There is a great advantage in providing this list of objectives to supervisors and designating this as the foundation on which to build an expanded and creative process of education. Supervisors often have areas of special interest and expertise that may or may not fit with the basic educational goals of an individual trainee or clinician. Starting with an outline of the core competency requirements helps focus supervisors toward a common goal. Providing the same list of goals to the supervisee means that both supervisor and supervisees will know from the outset what the minimal end product needs to be in terms of the knowledge and skills. Practicing clinicians will thus have a clear idea what their educational needs are as they meet with colleagues for supervision.

## SCHEDULED MEETINGS AND OTHER TYPES OF COMMUNICATION WITH THOSE WHO SUPERVISE

All of this, of course, requires a good process of communication with the supervisors. In today's world of ever-expanding network communication, it can take place by the means of the Internet, but those who supervise will benefit greatly from face-to-face group meetings. After all, supervisees and their supervisors need regularly scheduled meetings to discuss their cases. The same is true for supervisors in their work. Everyone's schedule is usually chock-full of obligations, but that is not a good reason to deny someone the opportunity to further his or her educational skills. Every time we schedule a meeting for those who supervise, it is well attended, and everyone is eager for more.

An educational agenda for supervisors could start with a discussion of psychotherapy competencies. Brainstorming together about how to best achieve the needed end result stimulates dialogue and usually leads to productive deliberations.

The demonstration of one of our seminars directed toward teaching clinicians about clinical case formulation has produced some lively interaction among the supervisors. An example of this was our use of the following format. In a course on psychodynamic psychotherapy and case formulation, the trainees watched a thirty-minute edited videotape of a patient that included a great deal about past history and interpersonal relations. Following this, the trainees wrote down possible clinical formulations, taking into consideration conflict and deficit theory, object relations theory, and attachment theory. Conjectures were made about anticipated transference and countertransference reactions. Once they had written and discussed their own ideas, they watched a videotape where an experienced psychoanalyst presented his formulations about this patient. In an evening meeting, we re-created the same experience for our supervisors. Meeting as a group, the supervisors walked through the same process. Their interaction, discussing possible case formulations, mirrored the experience of their supervisees and also created an opportunity for supervisors to engage with each other in an intellectually stimulating activity. This provided for enhanced learning and prepared the supervisors to better assist their trainees.

The next step in the residents' training is to have them write out and present to their colleagues similar expositions on their own psychotherapy patients. They are encouraged to ask their supervisors for assistance in developing these presentations. The supervisors, having joined together with colleagues in a similar process, understand the reasoning behind this endeavor and how to best assist the process.

## READING MATERIAL

A basic list of reading material for the supervisors is essential. It is natural for supervisors to have their own particular area of expertise and more familiarity with some theories of human behavior than others. However, to communicate effectively, there needs to be basic agreement about the terms we use. This is especially true when discussing psychotherapy. For instance, what is meant by supportive psychotherapy, and what are uniform expectations as to the goals of psychodynamic psychotherapy? There have been many papers written on the subject. Fortunately, the American Psychiatric Association has published a series of paperback books, edited by Glen Gabbard, on the psychotherapy competencies. The core competency books are currently available on supportive, long-term psychodynamic, and brief psychotherapy, and a book on cognitive-behavioral psychotherapy will soon be in the bookstores.[5, 6, 7] These books are small and inexpensive, and every supervisee and supervisor should own copies. The supervisees can use them to begin familiarization with the different processes. The supervisors, knowing the principles that are considered basic and essential, can use the information as a foundation on which to expand as the supervisees' process unfolds.

## PSYCHOTHERAPY GOALS

Education and a clear presentation of goals are particularly difficult tasks in the arena of psychodynamic psychotherapy. Frequently, the psychological processes that one is trying to influence cannot be seen or measured directly. The behavioral manifestations of an illness, such as the frequency of hand washing in a patient with obsessive-compulsive disorder, can be seen and directly measured. This is in contradistinction to concepts such as intrapsychic conflict, which must be hypothetically deduced from accumulated information. This makes it especially important to provide the bewildered young trainee with as clear an understanding as possible of psychoanalytic theory and the goals of treatment.

A helpful approach is to have trainees read and supervisors review McGlashan and Miller's article "The Goals of Psychoanalysis and Psychoanalytic Psychotherapy."[8] The authors, putting rivalries and personal attachments to particular theories aside, base their work on a survey of 192 books and articles and on their own clinical experience. From these sources, they culled what they considered to be the essence of treatment goals and the criteria by which to judge outcome. By identifying the goals of treatment, they also provide a critical step in defining the data by which to measure change, improvement, or regression. This work is particularly valuable because it is not limited to one particular frame of reference. Rather, it incorporates and integrates the concepts of various theoretical schools, including human development, the life cycle, self-concepts, object relations, and attachment theory. They identified eight different groupings or categories where one might look for change to occur: developmental, aspects of the self, object relatedness, fullness of experience, reality acceptance, integrative capacity, self-analytic functions, and symptomatology. The goal of the treatment might be to alter one or all of these categories, depending on the patient.

## ASKING THE RIGHT KIND OF QUESTION

Learning to ask the questions that will help the beginning trainee understand a patient's function in these areas is often a new process for the trainee. Schooled in the medical model, residents are skillful in making decisions about the patient's illness according to the *Diagnostic and Statistical Manual of Mental Disorders.*[9] However, they and similarly trained mental health professionals are often at a loss as to where to begin with a psychodynamic formulations. One way to start the learning process is to use the McGlashan Semistructured Interview, which has a special series of questions designed to answer these questions.[10] The trainees videotape the interviews and show the videotape to their psychodynamic supervisors. This provides the supervisor with a firsthand look at the patient under discussion. The supervisors, having understood the purpose of this task (they are sent copies of the various related articles), can actively assist the trainee in understanding how to piece together hypotheses about the patient's dynamic conflicts and the possible therapeutic goals and expectations as well as potential transference and countertransference reactions.

## SUPPORTIVE AND COGNITIVE-BEHAVIORAL PSYCHOTHERAPY COMPETENCY REQUIREMENTS

A similar process is in place to teach supportive psychotherapy and cognitive-behavioral psychotherapy. The appropriate supervisors are supplied with a list of the core competency expectations in these areas so that they have a firm understanding of the basic expectations for trainees.

Andrews and Burruss[4] outline the core competency expectations for supportive psychotherapy as follows:

1. Ability to identify defense mechanisms while supporting adaptive defenses
2. Ability to assume an active stance including ego lending and ego building
3. Ability to elicit and appropriately contain affect
4. Ability to employ crisis intervention techniques
5. Ability to utilize stress management techniques. (108)

For cognitive-behavioral psychotherapy, the expectations are the following:

1. Ability to set a collaborative agenda for each session, manage time limits, and foster the patient's eventual termination and self-management
2. Ability to help the patient recognize automatic thoughts, maladaptive assumptions, and core beliefs/schemas
3. Ability to identify and alter cognitive distortions in order to alleviate symptoms
4. Ability to help patients develop new, more rational responses to automatic thoughts and core beliefs
5. Ability to design and help patients plan and implement behavioral experiments such as activity monitoring with reward paradigms, in vivo exposure, and relaxation. (109)

Since there is a certain overlap in the areas presented, it is worthwhile to have the supervisors apprised of all these expectations.

## LIFELONG LEARNING

Physicians are well aware of the need for lifelong learning, as are many mental health professionals. Often it is not realized that the same is true for psychotherapy. If as psychoanalysts or psychodynamic psychotherapists we remained stuck in the era of Freud's topographical theory, we would clearly be archaic in our conceptualizations of mental conflict. Dialectic behavior therapy offers a splendid example of integration since it requires a behavioral approach combined with psychodynamic understanding to be most effective. Roth and Fonagy's new edition of *What Works for Whom?* answers many of the trainee's and neophyte clinician's common questions.[11]

Supervision of trainees and clinicians is an exciting and gratifying experience. It is one that continuously involves us in the process of lifelong learning. Becoming a better supervisor is a rewarding process and well worth the time and effort.

## NOTES

1. Marcia K. Goin and Frank M. Kline, " Supervision Observed," *Journal of Nervous and Mental Disease* 188 (1974): 208–13.
2. Frank M. Kline, Marcia K. Goin, and Wayne Zimmerman, "You Can Be a Better Supervisor," *Journal of Psychiatric Education* 2 (1977): 174–78.
3. Marcia K. Goin, Frank M. Kline, and Wayne Zimmerman, "The Use of Videotape in Teaching Supervision," *Journal of Psychiatric Education* 2 (Fall/Winter 1978): 189–96.
4. Linda B. Andrews and John W. Burruss, *Core Competencies for Psychiatric Education: Defining, Teaching and Assessing Resident Competency* (Washington, D.C.: American Psychiatric Publishing, 2004).
5. Glen O. Gabbard, *Long-Term Psychodynamic Psychotherapy: A Basic Text* (Washington, D.C.: American Psychiatric Publishing, 2004).
6. Arnold Winston, Richard Rosenthal, and Henry Pinsker, *Introduction to Supportive Psychotherapy: A Basic Text* (Washington, D.C.: American Psychiatric Publishing, 2004).
7. Mantosh Dewan, Brett Steenbarger, and Roger Greenberg, *The Art and Science of Brief Psychotherapies* (Washington, D.C.: American Psychiatric Publishing, 2004).
8. Thomas H. McGlashan and Glen H. Miller, "The Goals of Psychoanalysis and Psychoanalytic Psychotherapy," *Archives of General Psychiatry* 39 (1982): 377–87.
9. *Diagnostic and Statistical Manual of Mental Disorders*, 4th ed. (text revision). (Washington, D.C.: American Psychiatric Publishing, 2000).
10. Marcia K. Goin, Gordon D. Strauss, and Robert Martin, "A Change Measure for Psychodynamic Psychotherapy Outcome Research," *Journal of Psychotherapy Practice and Research* 4 (1995): 319–28.
11. Anthony Roth and Peter Fonagy, *What Works for Whom? A Critical Review of Psychotherapy Research*, 2nd ed. (New York: Guilford Press, 2005).

# 6

# Supervision of Boundary Issues

*Gail Erlick Robinson*

Every major professional medical and paramedical group has strict prohibitions against sexual abuse of patients. This includes not just sexual intercourse but also any type of sexual touching, kissing, or watching a patient or having the patient watch the therapist engage in any type of sexual behavior. Disciplinary actions range from being excluded from a professional organization (American Psychiatric Association) to losing a license to practice (College of Physicians and Surgeons of Ontario). Over nineteen states in the United States have made sex between a health care worker and a patient/client a criminal offense.

While didactic programs have little impact on potential predators, they can be invaluable in preventing the type of sexual misconduct that occurs because of the therapist's ignorance, neediness, or confusion of countertransference with love. However, many professional training programs do not provide specific teaching about boundary issues.[1] Even for those that do, the emphasis is often on sexual activity, ignoring other areas of potential boundary crossings, such as nonsexual touch, places and times of appointments, socializing, self-disclosure, language, gifts, rides, the use of power, and dual relationships. All this puts greater responsibility on supervisors to inform trainees about these issues and to deal with the specific events as they present during treatment.[2]

Supervision concerning boundary issues may take many forms. It may be part of the regular oversight of a student or trainee. A therapist in practice may seek out supervision from a more experienced professional as part of increasing his or her skills. A supervisor may be retained to meet the requirements of a disciplinary body after an individual has been found guilty of a boundary violation. In addition, the administrator of an institution or agency has a role in supervising the practices of all the staff. While the arrangements in each of these situations may be different, the basic teaching about boundaries remains the same. This chapter focuses first on supervising trainees and then discusses specific differences in other types of supervision.

## SUPERVISOR QUALITIES

As well as having clinical expertise, good supervisors are available, dependable, trustworthy, nonjudgmental, flexible, helpful, and available. As a teacher of boundary issues, the supervisor needs to have a solid knowledge of ethics and the appropriate disciplinary codes. Personally, the supervisor needs to have good personal boundaries and model proper ethical behavior. Whatever the discipline, the supervisor needs to have some basic knowledge of transference and countertransference, as it is problems in these areas that often lead to boundary violations.

Supervisors must abstain from sexual relationships with their supervisees. This is explicitly forbidden in the ethical codes of a variety of professional associations such as the American Psychiatric Association, American Psychological Association, National Association of Social Workers, and American Association for Marriage and Family Therapy, among others. This may mean that the supervisor walks a fine line as students and supervisors not uncommonly become very friendly. In fact, trainees often rate as their best supervisors those with whom they develop close relationships.[3] Authors suggest, however, that trainees who have had sexual involvement with their supervisors are more likely to become sexually involved with their own patients.[4] Certainly, if the supervisor is romantically involved with the trainee, it will completely interfere with the supervision. This may also occur if there is a possibility that the two of them might date. In such a situation, the supervisor may be reluctant to criticize the trainee for fear of ruining a current or potential relationship. Similarly, the trainee may not report what is truly going on with the patient for fear of being reprimanded or alienating the supervisor.

## WHAT THE SUPERVISOR NEEDS TO KNOW

### Definitions

Gabbard and Lester have defined boundaries as "the demarcation between the self and the object . . . the envelope within which treatment takes place."[5] Such boundaries provide "a flexible set of conditions that . . . [establish] an optimal ambience for the [therapeutic] work" and establish rules and role expectations that the patient may rely upon for safety required for treatment."[4] Gutheil and Gabbard have described boundaries as creating an atmosphere of "safety and predictability within which the treatment can thrive."[6] *Boundary crossings* are seen as "distinct, discussable departures from an established treatment framework."[7, 8]

These departures from commonly accepted clinical practice may or may not benefit the client. Ideally, a boundary crossing is something that has been carefully thought about on the part of the therapist and is designed to further the progress of the therapy. In contrast, *boundary violations* are departures from the usual practice that place the client or the therapeutic process in jeopardy.[7, 9]

## Etiology

Supervisors need to be sure that their trainees understand why boundary violations occur so that they can be alert to vulnerable situations. Health care workers may violate boundaries for many reasons.[7, 10, 11] They may be predators looking for opportunities to exploit a patient. They may be suffering from a disorder themselves (such as mania) that interferes with judgment. Some may not understand the difference between a professional and a personal relationship. Others may understand the risks of violating boundaries but do so anyway in a masochistic attempt to "save" the patient. Perhaps most commonly, the trainee believes that he or she has fallen in love with the patient and that this excuses boundary crossings. Trainees need to realize that, if their own lives are chaotic, lonely, or empty, they may unconsciously seek gratification from the patient.

Patients are also needy and vulnerable as they come for treatment when they are worried or in distress.[12] They want to please the therapist in order to avoid rejection. This may lead to their complying with—or even inviting—boundary crossings. Seductive behavior may be part of the patient's usual way of dealing with authority figures.[1, 13] They may initially see the boundary crossings as signs of being valued and special.[14] Even if the behavior is not welcome, the patient may be unable to refuse the advances, fearing that the therapist will become angry. In addition, transference reactions may lead the patient to believe that he or she is in love.

Boundary crossings and violations may occur as a result of the power differentials that exist in relationships between professionals and their patients.[13, 15] Clients see professionals as having the knowledge and wisdom to help them. The client is not trained to know when the therapist is crossing the line but tends to trust the therapist. The power differential is exacerbated by the fact that the professional gets to find out all about the patient while disclosing only what he or she chooses to. Trainees, especially when they are new, often have difficulty grasping the concept of a power differential in therapy. They may feel uncertain about out what they are doing and, therefore, not feel very powerful. On the other hand, they may not feel comfortable in their role as professionals and feel it is arrogant to assume they are more powerful. Trainees must appreciate that whatever their personal style, no matter what type of therapy is being used and even if they are feeling anxious and insecure about what they are doing, a power differential exists between the professional and the trainee.

A great deal of emphasis in discussing boundary violations has been put on the possibility of sexual contact between the patient and the therapist. There are a number of other boundaries that are important to maintain and need to be discussed in supervision. These include nonsexual touching, places and times of appointments, socializing, self-disclosure, language, gifts, rides, the use of power, and dual relationships. Even if the trainee never gets involved intimately with a patient, there may be violations of other boundaries that can lead to an impairment of the therapy.

The supervisor must also be aware of the risks of posttermination relationships, which may also be harmful to patients. Professional bodies have different views about the acceptability of such relationships. While some specifically prohibit them (American Psychiatric Association), others are silent on the subject. Some differentiate between the types of professional involvement. The College of Physicians and Surgeons of Ontario, for example, has a lifetime prohibition on relationships following any type of counseling involvement or when there has been an obvious dependency on the professional. When there has been a straightforward medical contact, such as seeing a patient for routine medical care, there must be a one-year interval between the end of treatment and the beginning of a personal relationship.

## Consequences

Trainees must also be taught that there are serious consequences to boundary violations.[13, 16, 17] The patient's initial problem may be not only ignored but also exacerbated. Patients may develop feelings of guilt, shame, mistrust, ambivalence, isolation, ambivalence, and anger. They may suffer from anxiety, depression, somatic complaints, or posttraumatic stress disorder. There may be an increased rate of hospitalization or suicide. The professional may suffer from shame, guilt, disgrace, and loss of license and profession. The relatives of the patient and the abuser may also suffer from confusion, shame, guilt, and a sense of betrayal. Other patients of the therapist also may feel betrayed, rejected, and angry and have a decreased sense of worth. The profession as a whole also may suffer from a decrease in the public's respect and trust.

## SUPERVISOR TECHNIQUES

Walker and Clark spoke about a number of major principles that allowed clinical supervision to support practice within ethical boundaries.[18] They noted that the supervision should be proactive rather than reactive; that is, supervision should be continuous rather than initiated only after some "disaster" in therapy. They also advised that the supervisor be sensitive to the supervisee's personal situation. If possible, the supervisor should be aware of significant changes in the supervisee's life that might indicate increased vulnerability. In addition, they commented that the supervisor must pay attention to the details of the supervisee's case and the interactions between clinicians and clients. They suggested that this could be done by regularly asking the supervisee to relate the full narrative sequence of clinical encounters. The supervisor should be alert to patterns or themes found in clinician–patient interactions. Finally, they advocated that the supervisory interaction include "guided exploration" rather than cross-examination.[19] They suggested that the supervisor use questions to "guide the supervisee to reveal and understand his or her clinical judgments and behaviors" rather than to interrogate the trainee.

The supervisor should establish a "milieu of safety and openness" in which learning can occur by offering a framework for the trainee.[20] Discussing the likelihood that feelings such as love, attraction, anger, impatience, and so on will be stirred up during therapy helps rid the trainee of fear of criticism or embarrassment that might interfere with the trainee's discussing these feelings in supervision.

Trainees need to understand the differences between feelings and actions. In addition, they need to be reminded that the type of feelings stirred up in therapy are related not only to the real-life experiences, hopes, and desires of the therapist and the patient but also to the factors implicit in the therapeutic relationship, in which the therapist is seen in an idealized manner and the patient in turn can become a source of immense gratification.

Obviously, discussing these feelings in supervision may result in some exposure of the student's personal life and intrapsychic issues. Here the supervisor needs to play a delicate role. It is important to encourage discussion of how the student's countertransference plays into these feelings without slipping into the role of therapist.[20] The supervisor cannot pressure the trainee for self-disclosure, as this may feel intrusive and threatening, thereby serving only to cut off any possibility of this happening. The supervisor also must not be critical of the trainee or jump to the conclusion that having feelings toward a patient is a sign of boundary problems on the part of the trainee. Similarly, the supervisor should not deny or ignore these feelings when they are expressed.

Ladany and Lehrman-Waterman have written about the supervisor's use of self-disclosure as an intervention technique to strengthen an emerging relationship in the beginning stages of supervision or to repair problematic supervisory relationships.[21] They discovered that when supervisors spoke about how they managed a certain kind of patient or specifically talked about dealing with a counseling struggle, the strength of the supervisory working alliance was increased. For example, the supervisor might share a recollection of when he or she crossed a boundary and how he or she handled it. Sharing counseling struggles implies a level of vulnerability of the supervisor and can serve as a form of modeling correct interventions as well as a powerful and important relationship-enhancing technique. The trainee gains confidence as he or she learns that all therapists must deal with self-doubt and countertransference feelings.

## DEALING WITH SEXUAL ATTRACTION DURING THERAPY

It is a common occurrence in therapy for the therapist to have feelings of attraction for the patient, including sexual and loving feelings.[20, 22, 23] The trainee who is not prepared for this may be overwhelmed by these feelings. The danger is that the trainee will either act on these feelings or withdraw into a distant, stunted, or restricted style of dealing with the patient in order to run away from these feelings. The supervisor has an opportunity to teach the trainee how to be comfortable with these feelings and learn how to manage them competently in both an ethically and a therapeutically sound manner. Rather than be frightened, the trainee can learn how to use these feelings in order to gain a better understanding of him- or herself and use them to benefit the treatment process.

**Case example:** Dr. W was treating a young male lawyer just a few years older than herself. He was a very charming and sensitive man. Through their meetings, she realized that they had many interests in common. It seemed obvious that he was also attracted to her. Dr. W found herself becoming more and more attracted to him as their sessions progressed. She did not say anything to her supervisor, as she thought that there was something wrong with her having these feelings of attraction. She thought that her supervisor would immediately tell her to end the therapy. As well as feeling that this would be harmful to the patient, she did not want to be in a position where she never saw him again. As the therapy continued and the young lawyer talked about his difficulty in finding a suitable partner and his loneliness, she felt herself further and further drawn to him. When the patient suggested that they meet for a drink after a session, Dr.

W rationalized to herself that this would help him open up more and agreed to it. Several meetings for drinks later, she found herself sexually involved with her patient. After an affair of several months, the lawyer broke off the relationship and reported Dr. W to her professional disciplinary body for exploiting him when he was vulnerable.

In this situation, the supervisor should have recognized the possibility of the therapist and client being attracted to each other. Had this been addressed as an almost expected part of the therapy, the trainee might have been able to recognize what was happening and identify the loneliness in both herself and the patient that was leading to their mutual attraction. The trainee could have been made aware of the fact that being attracted to the patient was not harmful or unusual; rather, not understanding this attraction and, therefore, acting on it became the problem. Discussing cases in which the supervisor became aware of erotic or loving feelings toward the patient and how they were handled not only provides a model of management for the trainee but also emphasizes that these feelings are normal and can be discussed in supervision.

Supervisors may have their own problems in addressing erotic transference or countertransference in therapy. Unless the supervisor refers to these feelings specifically, the trainee may hesitate to report them. Rather than understanding these feelings as common reactions to a patient, the trainee begins to feel that he or she has a special relationship with the patient. Therefore, these types of erotic and sexual feelings can bubble along in the therapy, potentially leading to boundary violations rather than being discussed at an early stage when they might be addressed and harm prevented.

Supervisors who become anxious when the trainee describes sexual fantasies or feelings give the message that these feelings are unacceptable. This will, of course, immediately squash any attempt on the part of the trainee to express or deal with these feelings. The supervisor must realize that having these feelings is not necessarily the first step of the "slippery slope"; rather, failing to acknowledge and deal with these feelings can be a source of problems. Supervisors can normalize the trainee's feelings as well as both support and encourage them by praising them for being able to recognize and bring these feelings up for discussion in the supervisory time.

The supervisor should start examining these feelings using a patient-focused approach. With this method, these feelings are looked at as coming out of the relationship between the therapist and the patient, in which a mixture of needs and experiences, both past and current, play a role. By looking at the reasons that the patient may be experiencing these feelings, it makes it a little easier for the trainee to talk about what is going on in the sessions. As the trainee becomes better able to tolerate this type of discussion, it may be easier to then shift to having the trainee look at his or her own role in the generation of the feelings.

> **Case example:** Dr. R, a first-year trainee, was becoming increasingly uncomfortable in his therapy sessions with Ms. B. With each session, she appeared to be more flirtatious. He found himself having fantasies about her. He felt very awkward about this but, instead of mentioning it to his supervisor, became colder and more distant in the therapy. His supervisor noticed the change in tone in the sessions and wondered whether it might be due to a growing sexual tension. Rather than confront Dr. R with this observation, he began speaking from his own experience. "This reminds me of the time I had a very seductive patient. I began to feel drawn to her myself." He went on to describe his experience, how he resolved his feelings and handled the therapy. This disclosure not only was helpful in terms of teaching techniques but also made the trainee feel it was okay to discuss his own sexual feelings in the therapy.

Although a minority of therapists advocate direct disclosure of therapist's sexual feelings toward a patient, it is not generally recommended. Such disclosures can be frightening to the patient, particularly when there is more concern about professional sexual misconduct. They may give the message to the patient that they should no longer talk about romantic feelings for fear that the therapist will see this as an invitation to act on them. Alternatively, they may seem like an invitation to the patient to expect that the therapist is looking for an intimate relationship. Although with some therapists there may be a way to discuss these feelings in a way that is helpful to the patient in order to help them understand the messages that are being transmitted, it is probably wise to recommend that trainees keep these feelings to themselves and to the supervisory process rather than discussing them with the patient.

## MANAGEMENT OF NONSEXUAL BOUNDARIES

Concerns about professional sexual misconduct have led to a tightening of boundaries. As a result, some therapists became very rigid in their approaches. Any type of boundary crossing was seen as a possible precursor to a boundary violation and the beginning of the slippery slope to sexual misconduct. More recently, there is a trend toward looking at boundary crossings as possibly being helpful to a patient when they are well thought out and considered for that individual patient and situation.[6, 18, 24, 25] Although this may make for better, more creative therapy, it does put added onus on the supervisor to train the supervisee how to assess a potential boundary crossing in order to ensure that the contemplated act will benefit the patient and the therapy. It is much easier to deal with a rigid system than to teach the judicious use of flexibility.

While there is zero tolerance for any type of crossing of sexual boundaries, the task in dealing with other types of boundaries is how to maintain creative flexibility in therapy without causing boundary violations. The therapist may use a boundary crossing in an intentional way to serve the needs of the patient or the therapy at that time. Awareness and attention to the patient's state of mind at a particular time and a willingness to bend the traditional rules to accommodate that need may be very beneficial to the therapy. The trick is to be able to recognize when such a crossing is beneficial or when it is the beginning of a slippery slope.

## Touching

One of the most common issues for trainees is the question of touching a patient. Most trainees feel comfortable with the idea of shaking hands at the beginning of therapy while appreciating that kissing or sexual touching is not appropriate or acceptable. The biggest question often has to do with hugging. While a hug is not necessarily the start of a slippery slope, the therapist must think carefully about the meaning in order to avoid problems. The types of questions suggested here serve as a model for analyzing boundary crossings.

> **Case example:** Ms. Z, a social work trainee, has been seeing a twenty-year-old student with relationship problems for the past four months. On one occasion, the student arrived at a session and began to cry. She reported that her father had been diagnosed with prostate cancer and was to have an operation. The patient was quite concerned about the outcome of this operation and the extent of the spread of the cancer. As she sat there crying, Ms. Z got out of her chair, sat down beside the student on the couch, and put her arm around the student's shoulders in order to give her a hug. The student did not protest or physically move away.

The therapist obviously wanted to console the patient, who may have felt that this was a very warm and human response. However, it is very important for the supervisor to discuss this scenario in detail and ask a number of key questions. Was the hug a routine part of therapy? If so, why? Was this an unusual occurrence? If so, why did the trainee choose to do it at this time with this patient? Would the trainee have done the same thing with another patient? Why did the therapist choose a hug rather than a touch on the patient's shoulder or hand? What was the reaction of the patient to the hug?

Although the therapist could see how the patient was physically reacting, what did the therapist know about the patient's emotional reaction to the hug? How much did the therapist know about the patient's past? Did the therapist know whether the patient had been sexually abused, had grown up in a family in which hugs were normal behavior, or had any subconscious lesbian attraction to the therapist or concerns about her sexual identity? How easy does the social worker think it would be for the patient to object to the behavior even if she felt uncomfortable? If the social worker wanted to offer comfort to the patient, what other options were there for this expression?

All these questions are designed to help the trainee think about her reasons for the behavior and the potential impact on the patient. Behavior that is harmful to a patient does not always start off as being harmful in the eyes of the therapist.[26] The therapist may have genuinely wanted to offer comfort to the patient. Many other, less intrusive methods are available, such as listening quietly, allowing the patient time to cry, sitting forward attentively, providing tissues, touching a shoulder or hand, or using a tone of voice or manner that indicates empathy. On the other hand, the therapist may have been trying to calm her own distress and feelings of helplessness at not being able to make things better for the patient. This kind of scenario gives the supervisor an opportunity to help the trainee understand that, even if a patient is uncomfortable, he or she might hesitate to say anything for fear of alienating the therapist. Therefore, one cannot count on the patient's speaking up if the behavior of the therapist is upsetting or intrusive. It is up to the therapist to think about the possibility of harm and not rely on the patient's ability to give feedback about unacceptable behavior.

The same questions apply to therapists who routinely give hugs at the end of a session. It is important that they question their policy of doing this routinely. Obviously, not every patient feels comfortable getting a hug from a stranger or even a therapist. Therefore, is the therapist meeting his or her own needs or that of the patient? The risk is that some patients may feel uncomfortable, while other patients may see this as an invitation to further intimacy.

Another aspect of hugging that may arise in a trainee's session has to do with the patient who requests a hug. The trainee may be confused as to how to handle the situation. He or she may worry about the patient's feeling rejected if the trainee does not acquiesce to such hugs. Once again, the therapist must try to determine the motivation for the hug. Is it a way of expressing thanks at the termination of therapy, just as the patient is departing? Does the patient ask for a hug on a regular basis, and, if so, what are the circumstances that usually create this request? Rather than just give in to the patient's demands, it is important to discuss the reasons for this request. Is this an attempt by the patient to seduce the therapist or hijack the therapy by initiating inappropriate contact? Even if this is a simple sign of appreciation, the therapist needs to think about whether it is necessary. Can a simple handshake suffice?

In some situations, the patient does not request a hug but, as he or she is exiting the door, suddenly reaches out to hug the therapist. Using physical defensive maneuvers to fend off these sorts of hugs may not be practical or wise. In such a situation, it is probably best to receive the hug without returning it. The therapist's body language can indicate that this is not in any way a romantic expression but merely the acceptance of a gesture of appreciation. After such a hug occurs, it is very important to discuss it in that or the next session. It is usually the therapist who will have to bring it up, as the patient may either not see any harm to it or may be embarrassed about giving the hug.

## Language

Trainees must also be aware of the impact of language on their patients. Clearly there is no place for erotic talk to a patient. This is different from the type of discussion one might have with a patient when doing sex therapy. There are other ways that language can be part of a boundary crossing. Commenting on an improvement in the patient's appearance may be legitimate if, for example, the patient is recovering from a depression and beginning to take more care with his or her grooming. Commenting on a patient's "sexy outfit" or "attractive body," however, is not appropriate. The trainee must be made aware of the fact that even if motivated by a wish to encourage the patient and increase the patient's self-esteem, these types of comments may rather make the patient uncomfortable or seem like suggestive invitations for a more intimate relationship. The language used may cross boundaries in other ways, such as being abusive and derogatory.

**Case example:** A forty-one-year-old family doctor was disciplined by his licensing body for unprofessional behavior. He was described by numerous patients as being frequently angry and abusive. He was quoted as referring to patients as "assholes" and telling a patient to "get the f____ out of my office." Despite his claim that he was overworked and exhausted, he received a six-month suspension of his license for conduct unbecoming a professional.

## Settings

As well as the length of sessions, trainees must be taught to think about the setting of sessions.[26] Certain therapies, such as behavior modification, may require that a therapist escort the patient out onto the street, into a restaurant, or into a store. It is very clear under these conditions, however, that the motivation is measuring the patient's anxiety and helping him or her to relax in a potentially stressful situation. This is very different from having lunch or a drink with a patient, even if the alleged purpose is to discuss the therapy. Such changes in venue may allow the relationship to slip into a more personal rather than professional mode. If the trainee suggests changing the location of the therapy, the supervisor must help him or her look into the reason for considering this move. If, for example, sessions always take place in the therapist's office, why would a therapist consider visiting a patient at home?

**Case example:** Dr. X had been seeing a thirty-five-year-old married woman for some time for assistance with the stresses of infertility treatment. The patient finally conceived, to the couple's great joy. This joy was, however, short lived when the baby died of SIDS at three months of age. The therapist met the patient regularly in the therapist's office. On this occasion, when the patient called to report about the death, she was very clearly upset. She and her husband were at home speaking with guests who had come over to help them mourn. On the patient's request, the therapist elected to go to the home. There the therapist met with the patient and her husband in a separate room to help them begin grief work over the loss of this child.

In this situation, although the therapy took place outside the office, the parameters were very clear. The therapist did not stay to speak with other friends or relatives or eat or drink at the home. The visit was very clearly a therapeutic one, done at the patient's residence with an understanding that the patient and her husband needed some instant support but that it was not feasible for them to come to the office at that time.

## Timing

If a patient is very distressed, the therapist may extend the session for an additional ten minutes to help the patient calm down before leaving the office. Extending this time on one occasion is very different from the therapist who gradually starts spending more and more time with the patient.

**Case example:** Dr. Y is was a psychiatric resident seeing an inpatient, Ms. B, for assessment and psychotherapy. The practice of the team was to do rounds on each patient every morning with the nursing staff. The trainee would then reserve a time during the day when he or she would meet with the patient for therapy. The usual practice was for the trainee to have a brief visit with the patient twice a week and a more formal therapy

> session three times a week. The nurses noticed that Dr. Y had begun meeting with Ms. B every day for sessions lasting forty-five to sixty minutes. After the patient had been in the hospital for several weeks, the sessions would sometimes go on for two to three hours in a day. Dr. Y also appeared at the hospital to see Ms. B in the evenings and occasionally on weekends when he was not on call.

Such a change in the therapeutic approach should certainly act as a warning sign to the supervisor, signaling that further investigation of the situation is required.

### Gifts

Trainees often have questions about gifts offered by the patient. A rigid approach would be to say that a therapist should never accept a gift from a patient. A sensitive supervisor will, however, understand that at times this might be insulting and rejecting of the patient. Trainees need guidance as to how to think about the issue of gifts. The supervisor can help the trainee think about why this person is giving a gift at this time. It is not unusual for patients to offer gifts at Christmas or when the therapy is terminated. This might be the patient's way of offering a simple "thanks" for the valuable assistance. Turning down such a gift might be more hurtful than helpful for the therapy. Of course, the trainee's decision also is based on type and price of the gift. A box of chocolates obviously has a very different connotation from lingerie. Gifts may be used to express a simple thank-you, to try to change the balance of power in the relationship by reminding the therapist that the patient has more money or influence, to make the therapist feel obligated to concede to the patient's demands for such things as a longer session or easier access to the therapist, or to test out the therapist's interest in changing the relationship to a personal one. A good supervisor of boundary issues can help the trainee think through whether a simple thank-you is enough of a response or whether the offered gift should be accepted or rejected after a discussion with the patient to help both more clearly understand the motivation.

Other "gifts" must also be similarly thought through. Accepting stock tips may leave the therapist in a difficult position if the tip is either a highly lucrative one or one that causes financial loss. Giving rides to or accepting rides from a patient places both in a situation where it may be difficult to retain a professional stance and the relationship becomes either very awkward or slips into more of a personal one.

### Self-Disclosure

Traditionally, therapists remained as anonymous as possible. Realistically, all therapists reveal a great deal of personal information via their style of dress, pictures of family in the office, and general office decor. Reexamination of the role of therapist self-disclosure has suggested that there may be times when careful revelations of a shared experience may be helpful to the patient. For example, to share with a worried, recently injured patient that the therapist recovered well from a similar injury may be very relieving. The therapist must be very careful to avoid any discussions of current stressors or very personal issues, as this might lead to role reversals in which the patient becomes protective of the therapist. The supervisor must help the trainee recognize the difference between helpful and harmful revelations.

## SUPERVISION RISKS

Walker and Clark discussed clinical supervision as "risk management."[18] The supervisor who is in charge of a trainee will also be responsible for that individual's work. If the trainee crosses boundaries, the supervisor will share in the responsibility. The client or patient relies on the supervisor to guarantee the quality of the treatment received.

> **Case example:** Dr. X was a second-year psychiatry resident seeing Ms. A in weekly therapy. He had weekly supervision from Dr. Smith. Dr. Smith did not introduce himself to Ms. A as was his usual custom. It was also the custom to videotape sessions for supervision; however, when Dr. X stated that Ms. A objected to this, Dr. Smith did not inquire further. Dr. X reported some attraction to Ms. A, who was his own age. Although Dr. Smith commented on the issues of countertransference, he did not pursue this in ongoing supervision. Nor did he comment when Dr. X pointed out Ms. A when she was leaving the clinic and remarked about how attractive she was. On one occasion, Dr. Smith met Dr. X and Ms. A at the entrance to the clinic, where Dr. X about to take a test-drive in Ms. A's new car.
>
> After five months of therapy, Dr. X finally reported that, in the last session, he had stated to Ms. A that he hoped they could be friends after the therapy ended. Dr. X appreciated that he should not have said that. The discussion about these comments and why they had occurred was fairly brief. Dr. Smith stated that perhaps he should join them in their next session; however, when Ms. A did not show up for the next appointment, he made no attempt to contact her to see how she was feeling or arrange a follow-up visit. He did not meet with Dr. X to talk about what had happened in the therapy and discuss the possible consequences to Ms. A. It was only when Ms. A phoned Dr. Smith complaining that Dr. X had been repeatedly telephoning her at home and asking to date her that he took any further action. Ms. A sued both Dr. X and Dr. Smith for mistreatment.

This vignette underlines some of the risks of being a training supervisor. In psychotherapy supervision, as opposed to other aspects of health care, the supervisor is not generally in the room monitoring what is going on. Instead, the supervisor has to trust that the trainee is accurately reporting what has gone on in the session. Trainees who are consciously or unconsciously contemplating crossing boundaries will not necessarily report their feelings or actions. Instead, they may selectively omit statements or actions that have made them feel somewhat uncomfortable or that they fear will earn the criticism of the supervisor. In a study of supervisees, Ladany et al. found that each averaged 8.06 nondisclosures to the supervisor.[3] The most frequent reasons were perceived unimportance, too personal, negative feelings, and a poor alliance. Supervisees make more disclosures to supervisors who are perceived to be open and collaborative.

There are a number of things that supervisors can do to help avoid problems for patients, trainees, and themselves. Routine examination of the trainee's progress notes or notes taken during therapy can be helpful. Although therapists seldom record information about crossing boundaries, the notes may indicate a therapy method that is different from what is being reported to the supervisor. There may be inadequate notes that do not support the treatment plan. If the notes deteriorate over the time the patient is in therapy, the supervisor should be concerned that something is going amiss in the therapy.

Forrest et al. suggested a number of rules for supervisors that would help ensure that their trainees are avoiding harming their patients or clients.[27] These include attending to the possibility that their trainees' personal problems might lead to the harm of others; attending to the possibility that trainees may misuse their influence; evaluating whether trainees are performing services responsibly, confidently, and ethically; articulating a clear set of professional standards; and evaluating trainees on the basis of these relevant and established requirements.

Supervisors must watch for any suggestions that countertransference issues are beginning to surface in the therapy. They must be aware of even the smallest types of boundary crossings and be willing to explore these. This may involve holding more complete discussions with the therapist, requesting video or audiotapes of several sessions, or observing the therapy either by sitting in or through a one-way mirror.[21] If the supervisor is really concerned, he or she might also speak directly to the client and explore the client's perception of the relationship with the therapist.

In the previously mentioned case, the failure to videotape the session, comments about the patient's physical appearance, and personal interaction concerning Ms. A's new car should all have been warning signals to the supervisor about possible boundary crossings. In and of themselves, they are not seriously harmful to the patient; however, because of the problem with lack of direct observation, they must be thoroughly explored with the resident in order to assess whether there are unconscious motivations to this behavior. Discussing these types of hints at an early stage may make the individual therapist more aware of the impending danger and, therefore, more careful about enforcing boundaries. Certainly, when it became obvious that a more serious boundary crossing had occurred (that is, the trainee's saying that he wanted a posttermination relationship), the supervisor should have taken direct action instead of allowing the situation to slide again. The supervisor needs to be aware of these issues in order to avoid harm to the patient as well as being held liable for the therapy that has gone wrong on the basis of negligent supervision.

**Case example:** In the case previously cited, Dr. Y began having longer and more frequent sessions with the patient. The nurses became concerned and mentioned this practice to the supervisor, Dr. Brown. Dr. Brown commented on this to Dr. Y but was reassured that Ms. B was just an interesting case, and so the matter was dropped.

Not only did Dr. Brown not see this change in the therapeutic approach as a warning sign, but he also ignored the feedback from the staff who were witnessing this new behavior, thereby putting himself at greater risk of being cited for negligent supervision. Similarly, if the patient begins to change in any way, this too should be explored. For example, the patient may start dressing in a different or more provocative manner, calling on a regular basis, or requesting to have sessions increased from weekly to daily. All these should be explored in detail with the trainee to assess whether these new behaviors illustrate a problem in the transference or countertransference.

## TRAINEE VULNERABILITIES

Good supervision is essential when there are any indicators that suggest the trainee may be at risk of committing boundary violations.[27] There may have been previous boundary violations or crossings that did not go through a formal discipline process. Trainees who demonstrate a marked and repetitive pattern of boundary crossings in the absence of self-observing capacity are at high risk of getting into trouble.[5]

Any trainee who is found to misrepresent his or her conduct in the treatment process should be seen as at risk of getting into difficulties. The trainee's attitude toward patients in general, as well as to other staff, might give indication that he or she is unsure of proper boundaries. A supervisor should certainly investigate any reports or suggestions by other staff that there is untoward behavior.

The junior resident might be the one most in need of supervision. During this time when the trainees are changing roles from a personal to a professional one, they may feel overwhelmed and inadequate. They may handle these feelings by trying to place the therapy on a more personal basis. For example, trainees may invite the patient to call them by their first name. Although the practice may be considered to be less intimidating and more friendly and comfortable for patients, it is important that it not be used as a way to blur the boundaries between the trainees' personal and professional identity. It is easier for trainees using their first names to minimize the power differential between the professional and the patient. In doing so, trainees fail to recognize their power over the patient. In turn, this may result in trainees' failure to recognize the possibility of abusing that power. They may look at the relationship as one in which the patient voluntarily consents or seeks out a relationship with the therapist rather than one that is governed by the patient's sense of vulnerability, idealization, and wish to please the therapist.

When trainees exhibit countertransference problems or have a personal history that makes them vulnerable to countertransference issues, it is very important for the supervisor to identify these and discuss them as sources of potential problems. It is also important for the supervisor not to cross the line between supervision and psychotherapy. The discussion of issues should relate only to problems in dealing with the patient and not get into a deep discussion of why the trainee has these problems. It might be necessary to recommend that the trainee undergo some personal psychotherapy if the issues appear to be deep seated and continue to interfere with the therapeutic work.

## PURCHASED SUPERVISION

According to the strict definition of supervision, the supervisor has control over and responsibility for the treatment provided by the supervisee. This is presumed to be the case in the supervisor–trainee dyad. In the case of purchased supervision, the supervisor does not have the type of access to the supervisee's files or the power to enforce any control over the treatment that is given. In this type of relationship, there is a danger in referring to it as "supervision," as this could result in the supervisors being deemed responsible for any treatment that is being provided. It has been suggested that, in this situation, the arrangement should be referred to as "case consultation."[28] Although the same knowledge base and supervision techniques may be used, this clarifies that the supervisor has no responsibility for or control over the treatment that is provided.

In case consultation, the private practitioner presents whatever cases he or she chooses in order to get advice and another perspective. Although the consultation may not have been sought specifically in order to address boundary issues, these may frequently arise. This type of consultation provides the opportunity to see the beginning signs of boundary crossings or countertransference weakening that may herald the risk of a boundary violation. Pointing out these problems early gives the practitioner a chance to avoid the slippery slope.

## REMEDIAL SUPERVISION

The supervisor may be specifically asked to offer remedial supervision to someone who is on probation or has committed an ethical violation.[29] Disciplinary or licensure boards often are not specific about the kind of supervision required but merely order that the member receive remedial training. An additional problem is that such supervision is often not voluntary.

### Prior to Agreement

Prior to agreeing to offer such supervision, the potential supervisor should obtain a thorough and detailed report about the nature of the disciplinary matter or the reason for probation. Such information is necessary in order to assess the suitability of the match between the supervisor and the supervisee and determine whether the nature of the offense is too personally troubling to the supervisor or would stir up so much countertransference that it would interfere with the supervision.[30] This information may later be compared with the story reported by the supervisee in order to get a sense of the individual's sense of responsibility for the actions that have occurred.

Once this information has been obtained, there are a number of issues to consider. If a remediation plan has been imposed, is it one that is practical and possible? Is the supervisor able to offer the hours needed to fulfill the task? Is the setting in which the supervisor works suitable for such an assignment? Is the selected supervisor qualified and knowledgeable enough?

### Planning

Once the supervision is agreed to, a plan must be set up. This may just be discussed, but it is preferable that it be written and agreed on by both parties and, where indicated, by the disciplinary body. It is important to clarify whether the supervision will be individual or group as well as to establish the frequency and duration of sessions.

The content of sessions should be decided. In the case of ethical violations, remedial work usually includes a review of the ethical guidelines, literature reviews, and, perhaps, discussion of various illustrative case vignettes. It must also be decided whether a certain amount of didactic material must be covered before the individual may resume seeing patients or patient care will continue during this time. The plan needs to also address whether all the individual's cases will be subjected to review. If not, how will the cases for discussion be chosen? This type of supervision requires more detailed process notes than those that are usually kept. The type of patient records required should be discussed as well as whether these will be reviewed regularly or at random. The supervisor must also decide whether regular video- or audiotaping of patient sessions will be required. Some supervisors find that this gives them a better sense of the atmosphere of the sessions as well as more detailed, less selective information. Decide whether review of records or tapes will occur before, during, or after supervision sessions.

In the case of an impaired professional, it is a good idea for the supervision to periodically include actual viewing of a patient session in order to avoid the risk that the supervisee is selectively reporting what has occurred in a session or failing to recognize the early signs of an impending boundary violation. This would usually be done using a two-way mirror. It may also include the use of an earpiece that allows the supervisor to give advice, comments, or feedback during the actual session.

The nature of the reporting duties must also be determined. The supervisor may be required to report at regular intervals to training programs or professional bodies. It should be clarified if a final report is necessary and what this should entail. The supervisor needs to know whether an opinion will be required as to whether the individual is fit to return to practice or should have any ongoing restrictions.

## ADMINISTRATIVE SUPERVISION

Administrative supervision involves oversight of professional work. In many agencies, the "administrative supervisor" does not actually do any psychotherapy supervision but is responsible for ensuring that clinical supervision occurs and ethical standards are upheld. This individual may be the one who completes evaluations as well as determining salaries, job descriptions, and so on. The administrator is responsible for setting policy in the institution. Future staff members should have their records reviewed to determine whether there have been previous problems with boundary violations. The administrator must make sure that supervision is available as necessary for all staff. There should be very clear prohibitions against boundary violations with a well-defined reporting system and enforced penalties. In Canada, there is an obligation on the part of the administrator of a facility to report to the appropriate disciplinary body if the administrator has reasonable grounds to believe that a member who practices at the facility has sexually abused a patient. The report must be filed within thirty days unless there are reasonable grounds to believe that the member will continue to sexually abuse other patients, in which case the report must be filed forthwith.

## BOUNDARY-CROSSING WARNINGS

Potential boundary crossings are impossible to avoid. Any patient may offer a gift, make an unusual demand of the therapist, or, by chance, meet with the therapist in a social setting. The good supervisor does more than advise on a particular situation; he or she also helps the trainee develop a way of thinking about these encounters or demands and, therefore, develop a way of deciding how to respond. The supervisor should also teach the signs that should alert the therapist as to the potential of committing a boundary crossing.[13, 18, 31] These include the following:

1. The therapist feels that he or she is falling in love with the patient.
2. Even without acknowledging feelings of love or attraction, the therapist realizes that he or she is looking forward to the next appointment with the patient.
3. The therapist realizes that he or she is dressing differently or paying more attention to grooming for that particular patient visit.
4. Without any request on the part of the patient, the therapist begins to book the patient habitually as the last appointment of the day, knowing that all the staff will be gone when the patient's appointment time is up.
5. Off-hours telephone calls are being made to or from patients.
6. Inappropriate gift giving is being done between clinician and clients.
7. Overdoing, overprotecting, and overidentifying is occurring with the patient.
8. Financial transactions other than the paying of fees are being conducted.
9. Personal disclosure of personal issues is increasing on the part of the therapist.
10. Physical contact is increasing between the therapist and patient.
11. The therapist begins considering a change in his or her usual practice, such as increasing the length or frequency of sessions, letting this patient use the therapist's first name, giving this patient a home telephone number when all other patients must use an answering service, considering meeting somewhere other than the office, and so on.

## KEEPING SAFE

There are a number of basic principles that the supervisor should impart to the supervisee. These principles should help the supervisee to think through a potential boundary crossing and avoid getting into difficulty:[13]

1. *Always be client/patient centered.* This principle reminds the supervisee that it is not enough to have good intentions for any actions done. Rather, it is important to think about how much the supervisee knows about how the comments or actions will be perceived by the patient. It is essential to always be aware of how much or little one knows about the patient's background, upbringing, conflicts, fears, fantasies, and current state of mind. In many cases, not enough is known to be able to predict how the patient will respond to what was intended to be just a comforting gesture. In that case, it is always wiser to take the safe route.
2. *Avoid risky situations.* Very often there is a safer alternative to a potential boundary crossing. A sympathetic posture and tone of voice, plus passing the tissues, can be a much safer way of consoling patients than putting one's arm around them. Why not choose the less risky alternative?
3. *When in doubt, check it out.* This does not necessarily apply to asking the patient how he or she feels about a particular action. Even if the patient feels uncomfortable about such things as the therapist offering a hug, patients who feel vulnerable and eager to please will find it very difficult to say no or express their discomfort. Rather, this implies the importance of ongoing case consultation. Supervisees should be advised that they should always feel comfortable talking in detail to a colleague about what has occurred in a session. If there is anything that they would hide or hesitate to disclose, they should examine what happened in the session and ask themselves why they feel uncomfortable letting another professional know.[26]
4. *The therapist is responsible for maintaining good boundaries.* Patients are not aware of proper therapeutic techniques. They naturally want to please the therapist. It is the professional who has the knowledge of potential harms to the patient and is, therefore, responsible for any boundary crossings or violations.
5. *Maintain a healthy and satisfying lifestyle.* If the therapist is overworked and overstressed and dealing with personal conflicts or strife, he or she becomes more vulnerable to looking for appreciation and gratification from the patient.[26] Just as a surgeon needs to keep his tools sharpened, the tools of psychotherapy include an ability to understand

one's own strengths and vulnerabilities and to be able to recognize when assistance is needed.

## CONCLUSION

Traversing and avoiding boundary transgressions is part of the daily work of the professional.[32] Boundary crossings, when well thought out and intentional, may be helpful to the process of therapy rather than being the start of a slippery slope. Boundary violations are always harmful. The good supervisor uses knowledge of the basic principles of boundary transgressions to help supervisees recognize and avoid serious problems. Rather than merely offering a set of prohibitions, the supervisor assists the trainee in developing ways of thinking about potential boundary crossings and spotting warning signs that help avoid disasters in therapy.

## NOTES

1. Greg E. Gorton and Steven E. Samuel, "A National Survey of Training Directors about Education for Prevention of Psychiatrist-Patient Sexual Exploitation," *Academic Psychiatry* 20 (1996): 92–97.
2. Cherrie A. Galletly, "Crossing Professional Boundaries in Medicine: The Slippery Slope to Patient Sexual Exploitation," *Medical Journal of Australia* 181 (2004): 380–83.
3. Nicholas Ladany et al., "Nature, Extent and Importance of What Psychotherapy Trainees Do Not Disclose to Their Supervisors," *Journal of Counseling Psychology* 43 (1996): 10–24.
4. Ken S. Pope, Hanna Levenson, and Leslie R. Schover, "Sexual Intimacy in Psychology Training: Results and Implications of a National Survey," *American Psychologist* 34 (1979): 682–89.
5. Glen O. Gabbard and Eva P. Lester, *Boundaries and Boundary Violations in Psychoanalysis* (New York: Basic Books, 1995).
6. Thomas G. Gutheil and Glen O. Gabbard, "Misuses and Misunderstandings of Boundary Theory in Clinical and Regulatory Settings," *American Journal of Psychiatry* 155 (1998): 409–14.
7. Leonard Glass, "The Gray Areas of Boundary Crossings and Violence," *American Journal of Psychotherapy* 57 (2003): 429–44.
8. David Smith and Marilyn Fitzpatrick, "Patient-Therapist Boundary Issues: An Integrative Review of Theory and Research," *Professional Psychology: Research and Practice* 26 (1995): 499–506.
9. Douglas Lamb, "Addressing Impairment and Its Relationship to Professional Boundary Issues: A Response to Forrest, Elman, Gizara and Vacha-Haase," *The Counseling Psychologist* 27 (1999): 702–11.
10. Glen O. Gabbard, "Sexual Misconduct," in *American Psychiatric Press Review*

*of Psychiatry*, ed. John M. Oldham and Michelle B. Riba (Washington, D.C.: American Psychiatric Press, 1994), 433–56.

11. Gary R. Schoener and John Gonsiorek, "Assessment and Development of Rehabilitation Plans for Counselors Who Have Sexually Exploited Their Clients," *Journal of Counseling and Development* 67 (1988): 227–32.

12. Nanette K. Gartrell et al., "Physician-Patient Sexual Contact: Prevalence and Problems," *Western Journal of Medicine* 157 (1992): 139–43.

13. Gail E. Robinson and Donna E. Stewart, "A Curriculum on Physician-Patient Sexual Misconduct and Teacher-Learner Mistreatment: Part 1," *Canadian Medical Association Journal* 154 (1996): 643–48.

14. Marlaina Sniderman, "A Counter Transference Problem: The Sexualizing Patient," *Canadian Journal of Psychiatry* 25 (1980): 303–7.

15. Ellen Luepker and Gary R. Schoener, "Sexual Involvement and the Abuse of Power in Psychotherapeutic Relationships," in *Psychotherapists' Sexual Involvement with Clients: Intervention and Prevention*, ed. Gary R. Schoener et al. (Minneapolis: Minneapolis Walk-In Counseling Center, 1989), 65–72.

16. Ken S. Pope, "Therapist-Patient Sex Syndrome: A Guide for Attorneys and Subsequent Therapists in Assessing Damage," in *Sexual Exploitation in Professional Relationships*, ed. Glen O. Gabbard (Washington, D.C.: American Psychiatric Press, 1989), 39–55.

17. Sameer P. Sarkar, "Boundary Violation and Sexual Exploitation in Psychiatry and Psychotherapy: A Review," *Advances in Psychiatric Treatment* 10 (2004): 312–20.

18. Robert Walker and James J. Clark, "Heading Off Boundary Problems: Clinical Supervision as Risk Management," *Psychiatric Services* 50, no. 11 (1999): 1435–39.

19. Tad G. Frantz, "Learning from Anxiety: A Trans-theoretical Dimension of Supervision and Its Administration," *Clinical Supervision* 10 (1992): 29–55.

20. Nancy A. Bridges, "Teaching Psychiatric Trainees to Respond to Sexual and Loving Feelings: The Supervisory Challenge," *Journal of Psychotherapy Practice and Research* 7 (1998): 217–26.

21. Nicholas Ladany and Deborah E. Lehrman-Waterman, "The Content and Frequency of Supervisor Self-Disclosures and Their Relationship to Supervisory Style and the Supervisory Working Alliance," *Counselor Education and Supervision* 38 (1999): 143–50.

22. Nancy A. Bridges, "Managing Erotic and Loving Feelings in Therapeutic Relationships: A Model Course," *Journal of Psychotherapy Practice and Research* 4 (1995): 329–39.

23. Nancy A. Bridges, "Meaning and Management of Attraction: Neglected Aspects of Psychotherapy Training and Practice," *Journal of Psychotherapy* 31 (1994): 424–33.

24. Thomas G. Gutheil and Glen O. Gabbard, "The Concept of Boundaries in Clinical Practice: Theoretical and Risk-Management Directions," *American Journal of Psychiatry* 150 (1993): 188–96.

25. Jerome Kroll, "Boundary Violations: A Culture-Bound Syndrome," *Journal of the American Academy of Psychiatry and the Law* 29, no. 3 (1990): 274–83.

26. Glen O. Gabbard, "Patient-Therapist Boundary Issues," *Psychiatric Times* 49 (2005), available at www.psychiatrictimes.com/p980301a.html.

27. Linda Forrest et al., "Trainee Impairment: A Review of Identification, Remediation, Dismissal and Legal Issues," *The Counseling Psychologist* 27 (1999): 627–86.

28. Gary R. Schoener and Ray M. Conroe, "The Role of Supervision and Case Consultation in Primary Prevention," in *Psychotherapists' Sexual Involvement with Clients: Intervention and Prevention*, ed. Gary R. Schoener et al. (Minneapolis: Walk-In Counseling Center, 1989), 477–502.

29. Gary R. Schoener, "Clinical Supervision: Ethical, Legal, and Practice Issues" (presentation given at University of Wisconsin, Madison, 2005).

30. Glen O. Gabbard, "Transference and Countertransference in the Psychotherapy of Therapists Charged with Sexual Misconduct," *Psychiatric Annals* 25 (1995): 100–105.

31. Larry H. Strasburger, Linda M. Jorgenson, and Pamela Sutherland, "The Prevention of Psychotherapist Sexual Misconduct: Avoiding the Slippery Slope," *American Journal of Psychotherapy* 46 (1992): 544–55.

32. Prudie Orr, "Psychology Impaired," *Professional Psychology: Research and Practice* 28 (1997): 293–96.

# III

# SO NOW I'M GROWN UP—DO I NEED SUPERVISION?

# 7

# The Supervision of a Psychiatrist-Manager

*Jacinta Powell*

As I sat down to write this chapter on supervision from the perspective of the psychiatrist-manager, I began to reflect on a situation that I had been called on to deal with recently. A trainee psychiatrist had been having some difficulties in terms of his communication, his documentation, and his clinical judgment, and my role was to talk to him and his supervisor about this. I showed him the documents that were the source of concern, gave him some feedback from the multidisciplinary team, and asked for his explanation. As he discussed his perspective, I listened and in my own mind interpreted what I thought was going on and had some sympathy for him, although there were clearly some defense mechanisms operating—denial, rationalization, displacement, and, at times, projection. At the end of the day, however, it was necessary to formulate a plan that would enable this trainee to improve his performance in assessment and management of patients. The approach taken illustrates the two processes that needed to occur in parallel to best ensure that a satisfactory outcome would eventually ensue—either the trainee would improve and meet the expected standard or he would reconsider his career choice. As a manager, a performance management approach was implemented with the areas for improvement clearly identified, the supports that would be put in place to enable this to occur, and a time frame for review. As a psychiatrist, I recognized the pivotal role that supervision would play in the development of the trainee's clinical and interpersonal skills. While we expect trainees to be involved in supervision, increasingly we have come to realize that learning and development as a psychiatrist (or indeed any specialist medical practitioner) is a lifelong process. The agencies and the patients that employ our skills are beginning to demand that we demonstrate safety and quality in our practice. I would argue that regular supervision encourages reflection and self-examination of our clinical practice, a process integral to continuous quality improvement.

## SOME BACKGROUND

### The Decision to Become a Psychiatrist

As a child, I went through phases of ever-shifting career plans; as a medical student, I was going to be a plastic surgeon; as a psychiatry resident, my future practice was to be in the private sector. However, I am none of those things: for about ten years, I have been a psychiatrist and manager in the public health sector.

In early medical school, my career aspirations tended to shift on a regular basis, depending on what the subject was and which term I was undertaking. Good experiences in practical terms and contact with teachers would fan my interest in a diverse range of topics. Undertaking a term in psychiatry in fifth year was something of a revelation. For the first time, there was a focus on the whole person, not just a segment of one's anatomy or bodily system. Each person had a story that was unique. The stories were an interweaving of the individual and his or her interactions with the world.

Entering my postgraduate years, I maintained an interest in both psychiatry and surgical specialties. A decision had to be made, and in the end practicality prevailed. Gaining a much-sought-after place on the surgical training program at the time required at least two more years in a nontraining position. In addition, a number of people had just been ejected from the surgical program after working long and unsociable hours for the requisite years and female surgeons were a rare breed. On the other hand, I could enter psychiatry training immediately, the training program was well supported, the psychiatrists were encouraging and approachable, and role models abounded.

Psychiatry training was conducted largely in the public sector. The Royal Australian and New Zealand College of Psychiatrists (RANZCP) set down the curriculum and training requirements. Trainees were employed by public hospitals and community mental health clinics. Successful completion of training requirements and examinations would result in the conferring of a fellowship that would enable recognition by the registration board as a specialist psychiatrist. Training was conducted in six monthly rotations requiring considerable experience in general adult and acute psychiatry with six-month terms also in child and adolescent psychiatry and consultation liaison psychiatry. Weekly individual supervision with a specialist psychiatrist was a requirement of training.

Changing terms every six months was not conducive to longer-term therapeutic relationships and hence psychotherapy. In addition, public hospital psychiatry tended to be limited to the more severe and chronic mental illnesses. However, training requirements included the need to undertake the care of one person with psychodynamic psychotherapy for at least fifty sessions. During the course of my training, I undertook such therapy with four patients for varying periods ranging from a few months to two years. I obtained specific psychotherapy supervision, as was required, to develop my skills in this area. This supervision was by a psychotherapist with a group of three or four trainees and could best be described as eclectic. While feedback regarding my own interactions with patients was useful, it was highly beneficial to be privy to the experiences of other trainees.

The end of my five-year training course culminated in a year spent in a private psychiatric hospital as a senior resident. This represented a considerable shift from the public sector in terms of both organization and the issues with which patients presented. During this time, I worked extensively in the eating disorders unit of this hospital and undertook work with private outpatients with anxiety and depressive disorders under the supervision of a range of experienced psychiatrists and other health professionals.

## A Junior Consultant

However, once I obtained specialty qualifications, I returned to the public sector and a large teaching hospital in an inner-city area as a junior consultant in a general adult ward looking after both inpatients and outpatients. Employment conditions enabled continuation of a limited private practice on campus. My plans at this stage were to work in the public sector for about three years before moving to private practice. Within a short period, an opportunity was thrust on me to take on an administrative role, a situation that has continued to this day. My interest in people's stories continued, but eventually working with individuals only wasn't enough. I wanted to understand the bigger picture and how a difference could be made by taking a systems or global perspective. This led me initially into setting up an eating disorders service and then moving on to become the director of an integrated mental health service for an inner-city population of about a quarter of a million people.

All these decisions were significantly shaped by a series of mentors: those who initially encouraged me to take up psychiatry, then those who developed my subspecialty interests, and finally those who supported me in undertaking new roles. These included supporting me to obtain management qualifications and providing support and supervision while I learned how to apply these new skills. Underpinning these changes was contact with patients—as I would learn their stories and come to an understanding of how they came to be where they were, I began to wonder about how different things might have been for them if the systems in which we live and work were different.

Seeing a young man with schizophrenia who has a criminal history and no accommodation, one is struck by the limitations of individual therapy with this man. The importance of having responsive flexible systems that enable him to get a roof over his head and a source of income and support to reconnect with his family and to stop using drugs and help him take his medication is evident. Casting a wider net makes one consider what might have been if an intervention while he was still a boy would have recognized the risks of his birth into a family with a history of mental illness and substance abuse and his struggles with learning difficulties at school. Considering these issues leads to thinking about how resources are limited and how government services are often bureaucratically inflexible.

## THE ROLE OF THE PUBLIC SECTOR PSYCHIATRIST

Boyce and Tobin[1] divide the role of the public sector psychiatrist into clinical and managerial: the former revolving around the care of patients and the latter around the organization in terms of human resource management, advocacy for patients, and service planning. Of note is that they identify roles for the psychiatrist beyond clinical leadership via individual patient care, discussing the need to demonstrate clinical leadership in a variety of ways via supervision, accountability, complex assessment skills, and shared management of complex and difficult patients. Direct clinical care is identified as being vital to demonstrating clinical leadership in terms of development and maintenance of skills and job satisfaction. It is necessary for the public sector manager to be a model for staff and colleagues. "Management should no longer be seen as an eccentric hobby for the bored or inept doctor" (1636).[2] While needing to be up to date in clinical skills in order to supervise other staff, the manager should be prepared to take on the care of some difficult cases and be prepared to assist staff in undertaking the assessment and management of others.

My public clinical work includes working in a multidisciplinary team with allied health professionals, nurses, and residents, providing care to people with a spectrum of problems. These include mostly chronic and severe mental illness complicated by substance abuse, limited social supports, and very basic accommodation and employment options. While community mental health services are gradually being better resourced, there remains a mismatch between demand and what can be provided. In particular, there is a lack of disability services and accommodation options for those with chronic mental illness, hence limiting the effectiveness of the mental health care being offered. Mental health professionals spend considerable time trying to assist people into accommodation, which is limited in scope, suitability, and availability. Integration and continuity of care were key tenets of the Australian National Mental Health Strategy 1992.[3] Hence, as a clinician, my role is to care for patients on the inpatient unit with clinical staff and then continue this care on the patients' discharge into the community. In an inner-city public mental health service funded by the state government, the patients tend to be at the severe end of the spectrum. Most suffer from chronic and severe psychotic disorders, often with substance abuse issues, and some also have coexisting personality disorders or traumatic brain injury or intellectual disability. Comorbidity and complexity is the rule rather than the exception. In addition, there is a small but significant group of people with severe behavioral disturbance in association with either borderline or mixed personality disorder.

The inpatient units are two twenty-five-bed adult acute wards with patients allocated according to geographical location in the catchment area. These correspond with the two continuing care teams. The continuing care teams are staffed by allied health professionals (AHPs; occupational therapists, psychologists, and social workers) and nursing staff with an operational reporting line to a team leader (either a senior nurse or AHP) and professional reporting line to a senior member of the same profession. Caseloads are approximately thirty per case manager with the exception of three staff per team who undertake assertive case management (caseload of eight to ten) with people identified by the early psychosis program. As a teaching hospital, the service provides training for medical, allied health and nursing students, medical house staff, and psychiatry residents. Entry to the service is via the acute assessment services through either the psychiatry emergency center, adjacent to the hospital emergency department, or the community mental health site. A twenty-bed community care unit operates to provide intensive rehabilitation for those people unable to survive in the community with conventional levels of support.

While I undertake my clinical work with a continuing care team and the associated ward, my managerial role is to undertake the operational management of the entire integrated mental health service as detailed previously. This includes service planning, organizational and human resource management, and delegated budget responsibilities. All these tasks are undertaken with the assistance of a divisional director, nursing director, business manager, team leaders, and consultant psychiatrists. While I may like to think that such skills come naturally, they are in fact a developing work in progress. Several authors suggest that while some characteristics of psychiatrists assist them in managerial roles, there is a risk of hindrance through a tendency to interpretation and consultation rather than providing clear direction when needed.[4, 5]

## MENTORS

As previously discussed, I have been fortunate to have a series of mentors. Through the guidance of my most recent mentor, I was able to develop skills and identify a path of study to initially attain a graduate certificate in management and, later, a master's degree in health administration. The role of this mentor is consistent with that described by Roberts et al. as a "confidential, professional and supportive relationship, by an experienced colleague, able and willing to share his or her knowledge and experience" (107).[6]

## SUPERVISION

As my mentor was an experienced psychiatrist-manager, the focus was on developing managerial skills. However, I felt that there needed to be a similar process available for the development of my clinical leadership. During the course of my training, it was mandatory to undertake at least one psychotherapy case with appropriate supervision. This process was then submitted as a case study to the RANZCP, in a deidentified form, for assessment. Trainees are still required to submit case studies over the course of their training that provide evidence for experience in not only psychodynamic psychotherapy but also other therapeutic modes, including cognitive-behavioral therapy. It is common for psychiatry trainees to seek supervision for therapy cases with psychiatrists and psychologists outside the health system in which they are employed. Some of these supervisors are in the private sector, where there is considerable expertise particularly in psychodynamic psychotherapy. Having a tendency to discuss difficult cases and situations with colleagues who I felt worked in a similar manner to myself, we often found that we tended to see similar types of patients and unsurprisingly struggled with similar transference issues. As a result, one colleague suggested that we seek psychotherapy supervision as we did as trainees. This seemed quite sensible and would fulfill my need to develop my clinical skills. The choice of supervisor was fortuitously made simple by the arrival of an experienced psychotherapist from overseas at about that time.

As Rose and Boyce note, the emphasis in supervision of psychiatrists is on "refining and honing clinical skills that will lead to more effective management of patients and resources, as well as an opportunity to develop collegiality and peer support" (11).[7] As a result, I have been part of a supervision group for a number of years, and we see our supervisor, a senior psychiatrist experienced in psychodynamic therapy, on a regular basis from every other week to monthly. The group has had a stable core of three, with each working in a different context. My recollection is that the decision to be involved in group supervision rather than individual was not too difficult, perhaps because I had previously had experience with group supervision as a trainee, I was working in the public sector and presenting cases with variable outcomes at educational forums, and I had discussed cases with the other group members on a regular basis. Despite my familiarity with the group, there remained some initial apprehension about discussing my clinical practice, particularly the countertransference reactions. I had some fears about exposing potential gaps in my knowledge and admitting inadequacies in my psychodynamic understanding and responses. While such fears are understandable when being supervised by someone perceived as having superior knowledge, the fears were magnified by the presence of peers witnessing the process of my supervision. On the other hand, being able to observe other psychiatrists presenting cases and being supervised was a powerful learning experience.

Initially, we all focused on presenting individual patients with significant psychodynamic issues, often when we were struggling to see a way forward or having difficulties with countertransference. However, over time, as my work roles and personal circumstances have changed, so too has the range of issues that are discussed in supervision. Examples include team dynamics, ward milieu, or how best to manage a situation with a colleague. The latter issue of the altered and uneasy relationship between doctors and the doctor-manager is well described in the literature.[8, 9, 10]

**Case example:** I had set up and managed the eating disorders service for about five years, adding the oversight of some other campus-based services and registrar coordination in the latter part of that period, when I was approached to move into the role of director of the integrated mental health service. My colleagues who worked in that service talked to me about how they were looking forward to this, as they thought that this would be very beneficial since I was younger and female and could bring a fresh perspective to changes that were occurring in that service. On my first day, my first task was to chair the weekly meeting of community-based staff. Armed with the minutes of the previous week but little else, I fronted up, attempting to look as if I knew what I was doing. An agenda item arose regarding changing patients from accessing medication at no charge to giving them external prescriptions that they could take to any pharmacy; most would have to pay a concessional fee for each item. A senior colleague spoke up saying that he thoroughly disagreed with this change and asked me my opinion. I looked around at the dozens of curious faces of a myriad of clinical staff whom I did not yet know, aware that

> I was being tested and was about to be found wanting. I said something about looking into the matter and went on with the meeting. The change went ahead despite the considerable anxiety expressed by some staff who felt that patients being treated involuntarily under the mental health act should not have to pay for their medication. The patients coped with the change remarkably well despite the reservations of the staff, and in fact one could argue that the change was beneficial, as the power dynamic between patient and service provider shifted a little toward greater patient autonomy through normalization and personal responsibility.

This scenario was a taste of things to come when my job required me to make management decisions that impacted on my colleagues. Some decisions had an indirect effect that were perceived to diminish clinician autonomy; others directly affected the jobs of individual clinicians as a result of a shift in where services were required or the performance of the clinician. Experience, further study, mentoring, and supervision have improved and developed my ability to anticipate and manage such reactions. It is in supervision that I can look at the dynamics of what is occurring, the issues that I bring to the table in such encounters, and this also allows me a debriefing opportunity. Self-awareness and understanding of human motivation and behavior provide a valuable adjunct to contemporary human resource management when one is aware of the pitfalls of confusing the managerial role with the clinical one.

## SUPERVISION OF OTHER MENTAL HEALTH PROFESSIONALS

While working closely with other mental health professionals, I became aware of their supervision requirements. The community case managers were from four different professions: social work, occupational therapy, psychology, and nursing. Supervision of their clinical practice was an expectation of contemporary practice and was undertaken by a senior member of the same profession. During my tenure as the director of the service, a policy of mandatory supervision was introduced at a state level. This policy included the need for a supervision contract and responsibilities of each party involved. However, while such supervision of clinical practice is a component of ensuring that clinicians are providing service appropriately, there was an obvious lack of a forum to discuss psychodynamic aspects of the therapeutic relationship. Such issues would sometimes be raised during an ad hoc difficult case conference or an educational session. However, the approach was inconsistent, and it was apparent that a proactive approach to reviewing therapeutic difficulties might be beneficial in terms of supporting staff, reducing burnout, and modeling the concepts of psychodynamic work with the presentation of cases regularly. As a result, after discussion with the community mental health staff, a monthly supervision session was introduced. While I undertook the initial role as supervisor, an opportunity arose shortly thereafter to employ a senior psychiatrist, experienced in psychodynamic therapy, on a sessional basis. The hour-and-a-half sessions are very popular with staff with an attendance of about twenty to thirty people. Each session covers one case usually presented jointly by the case manager and treating doctor. Having an external facilitator offers the potential for a fresh perspective and a reduction in staff discomfort, as they are no longer presenting their work for direct scrutiny by myself as their line manager. The sessions are conducted with the principles of confidentiality and respect for presenters clearly spelled out on a regular basis. Staff are encouraged to reflect not only on their individual reactions to the patients they treat but also on how they would respond to those who are presented. Participation is voluntary both in attendance and in terms of exposing one's feelings. Expressed feelings are then used to illustrate particular aspects of the psychodynamic process.

A similar process would be very helpful for the inpatient unit nursing staff. However, available resources and staff shortages limit access to all forms of offline education for ward nursing staff. The employment of a senior nurse on a part-time basis, purely to provide nursing supervision, is a step in the right direction. This does allow some flexibility in terms of delivery, a necessity for such an acute service with unpredictable demands.

All patients of the mental health service have an assigned doctor: either a psychiatrist or the trainee they are supervising. In addition, the majority of patients also have a case manager. A significant portion of the psychiatrist's time is spent supervising others, their particular trainee, case managers, and other staff. This occurs both formally in scheduled supervision sessions for trainees and in ward rounds and three monthly case reviews for other staff. Informal supervision through corridor discussions is arguably the most common form of supervision within the mental health service.

## A BROADER PERSPECTIVE

After three years as the director of the local mental health service, I was approached to undertake a temporary move into the state government mental health unit as principal adviser in psychiatry for eighteen months. This was followed by a six-month term as the state director of mental health. This temporary appointment allowed me to develop an understanding of mental health policy at a population level, the process of funding acquisition for mental health services, and the statutory responsibilities associated with the state mental health act. In addition, the role incorporated the provision of clinical expertise and advice to the government. This allowed me to experience firsthand the potential benefits that could be brought about through a more global role but also brought me closer to the constraints and barriers to bringing about the benefits.

For example, in my previous role, I had undertaken a therapeutic role with two women with severe personality disorders associated with dangerous behaviors. This included coordinating their care, providing supervision to the assigned case managers, convening difficult case conferences, and providing direct supportive therapy to the women themselves. When I became aware that I would be changing jobs temporarily for at least a year, I knew I would have to make a decision about what to do about these two patients. I could hand their care over to other psychiatrists in the service, although this would not be easy. However, I could also continue to see them for ongoing therapy, as I was continuing my limited private practice on campus during the temporary appointment, while my replacement could take on the role of care coordinator. The decision was not a straightforward one. My feelings about the patients were mixed. On the one hand, they were both relatively likable, and when I originally took them on, it was in the knowledge that these would be long-term ventures. On the other hand, they were the source of frequently expressed frustrations by the many people they came into contact with as a result of disturbed behavior—the police, the emergency department, the community, and other mental health professionals. Hence, along with the other mental health workers involved, I would spend considerable time attempting to contain those that they came into contact with while at the same time grappling with my own sense of impotence and failure.

I had presented both these patients to my supervisor previously and decided to again do so in the context of making a decision about what to do. By considering taking them into my private practice, was I succumbing to a grandiose belief that only I could help them? On the other side of the coin, I secretly hoped that my supervisor would agree with this premise and I could legitimately then pass them on to someone else with a reduced sense of guilt. Being able to recognize and name the processes of projective identification and psychotic transference only alleviated my discomfort to a limited extent when I was "being with" these patients and experiencing a little of the affects and self-loathing with which they lived. At this time, I had been involved in group and individual supervision for some years and felt comfortable discussing my feelings about patients both with my supervisor and in front of the other two participants. The upshot was that the supervisor pointed out that I already knew what to do: to continue undertaking supportive therapy with both patients in recognition of the importance of the long-term need for continuity and persistence with such patients who have mixed personality disorders with borderline features.

Throughout my two years in the statewide mental health administrative roles, I continued to attend supervision sessions, although my own clinical practice was with a handful of such private patients. The sessions allowed me to stay in touch with clinical practice issues with the presentations of the other two psychiatrists. However, I was also able to use this contact to discuss ethical and systemic issues related to service delivery and decision making.

The state had a large health bureaucracy, as decisions regarding the organization and funding of health services including hospitals and community health services were made centrally. As previously noted, a major component of the principal adviser role was providing information and opinion to the government and the health department hierarchy. The role provided clinical psychiatric input into policy development as well as advising the government and the senior health department bureaucrats in relation to serious incidents, media scrutiny, and complaints. As a result, I became involved in an ad hoc process of reviewing major incidents and writing reports for district health services and senior health officials. This was generally a difficult and uncomfortable process, as one needed to temper the identification of problems with the knowledge that I was operating with the benefit of hindsight. The intent of incident analysis was to identify system errors and make recommendations about changes to practice and processes that would reduce the risk of such a recurrence. Reason divides the approach to human error into either a person approach or a systems approach. In the former, the focus is on "unsafe acts" viewed generally as arising from individual aberrations and hence resulting in responses that exacerbate people's fears of being shamed, exposed, and sued. The latter, the systems approach, recognizes that "humans are fallible and errors are to be expected, even in the best organizations." The response then required is to change the environment in which humans work and build in system defenses.[11] Considerable effort now goes into assisting health care professionals understand patient safety and the need for reporting incidents. Unfortunately, clinicians struggle to speak about their errors to their colleagues and often see "error as a failure of character" (1851).[12]

**Case example:** The suicide of a young man just after admission to an inpatient unit demonstrated the tragic consequences of a series of errors, any of which on their own or in a different combination would have likely led to a very different outcome. However, in the absence of a robust system of "defenses, barriers and safeguards" (769),[13] a cascading series of errors resulted in the untimely death of a young man with his first episode of psychosis. In this case, there were examples of error-inducing deficits in the workplace, including understaffing due to planned and unplanned absences, time pressures, lack of experience, and supervision. This was combined with long-term weaknesses in the defenses, including ward design and construction deficits, unclear policies and procedures, and inadequate role definition. The staff involved were very traumatized by the experience, some were shouldering considerable self-blame, and all were fearful of being named, shamed, and exposed to litigation. The investigation and subsequent report was designed to identify and recommend action to close the holes in the system. This occurred shortly after this young man's death and was considerably aided by a grieving family who, while understandably distressed and angry, strongly expressed their wish that the system be improved rather than anyone be punished to try to prevent any other family going through what they had. Contact with my supervisor, my mentor, and senior respected colleagues enabled me to be with the staff and the family and to navigate the inherent tendency toward individual blame, which, as Reason notes, is "more emotionally satisfying than targeting institutions" (770)[14] and steer the report to an outcome that attempted to meet the needs of the family, individual staff, and the organization.

Halfway through my two-year temporary appointment, a major life event occurred. I became pregnant, fortuitously being due to deliver about three weeks after the director of mental health was expected to return to resume her position. Supervision at this stage was focused on when and how to disclose this event to my patients, particularly those with borderline personality disorder. The situation was made more difficult, as I did not wish to disclose my state to my colleagues until the results of amniocentesis were available at about sixteen weeks. Trusting the confidentiality of supervision, during a session when the other group members happened to be unavailable, I discussed that I felt it was necessary to raise my impending absence with my patients before the pregnancy was obvious. However, I had to anticipate each individual's reactions and develop a therapeutic approach for each. Of particular concern was a patient of many years whom I had been working with in a psychodynamically informed way to contain her risk of self-destructive behavior and to help her sustain her relationships and functioning in the community. Her defenses were highly primitive, and she struggled to self-soothe. She tended to become reliant on others, including various mental health professionals, for containment. Helping her toward developing boundaries, delay gratification, and use cognitive strategies when in crisis had taken many years. Therapy with this woman was akin to "having the tiger by the tail" as described by Briere when discussing therapy for people with a history of severe abuse. His description of therapy with such people entailed hanging on and staying with the client "until she is through with what she has to do—no matter how uncomfortable the ride may be for the therapist" (152).[15]

I had presented this woman to my supervisor on a number of occasions previously; hence, the supervisor was already well aware of the dynamic issues that repeatedly appeared in therapy. I had many concerns about how and when to tell this patient. How would she respond, and how much could I endure during this time before I went on leave? I had some fear for my own safety and that of the baby. To whom could I refer her while I was away? I was aware that I did not really wish to allow the patient into my world. I realized, with the assistance of supervision, that part of the work with this patient had been to hold firm boundaries empathically, therapeutically, in the face of repeated attempts at intrusion.

Now, together with the patient, I had to renegotiate the boundaries. My pregnancy was inalienable evidence of sexuality and visibly confirmed that I had other relationships. She had always quizzed me about my other patients in an attempt to convince herself that she was special to me and that really I had only a relationship with her. The transference was ever shifting and required constant vigilance. Now a new, difficult-to-ignore threat was about to intrude into our relationship. Regular supervision offered stability and insight that assisted me in responding to the stormy period that followed. Sessions with the patient were characterized by verbal abuse, derogatory sexualized remarks, and distressed pleadings. Her initial response on being told of my maternity leave (about four months away) was disbelief. She stated that pregnancy was impossible, as "you must be at least sixty!" Describing the details of the sessions that followed is beyond the scope of this chapter. However, aspects have been well described by many other pregnant therapists.[16, 17, 18] Both patient and I survived this trying time. Before I returned to work, I undertook further supervision to enable me to deal with the issues that would arise. I returned after six months of leave to find that this patient had booked the first appointment.

## SUMMARY

Supervision has been a work in progress for many years now. Initially, presentations were very patient focused with direct assessment and treatment issues discussed. Some were psychodynamically focused for those patients in ongoing therapy, but others were about reviewing diagnosis and management. Over the years, the patient presentations have become briefer and more focused on core issues. However, we regularly revisit the work we are undertaking with patients, especially those with a borderline personality disorder. At times, other health professionals who are involved in the care of particular patients are included in a supervision session. Mostly the group continues with the three of us and the supervisor, each session having one, two, or three attending.

During this time, we have developed greater self-awareness and are more confident in providing input in cases other than our own. We have increasing confidence and trust in each other, enabling us to expose uncertainties, fears (rational and irrational), and feelings about patients. There has been a broadening of the supervision scope, particularly for me, as my practice changed from predominantly direct patient care to involvement in state and national mental health systems development. I have also been able to use supervision to raise my concerns about people management issues, ethical dilemmas, and systemic issues for mental health service delivery, including the supervision of consultant psychiatrists in the public sector and my changing relationship with colleagues.

While supervision has been demonstrated to be an effective training method and therefore a component of continuing professional development, there has been little research to demonstrate the concept that supervision results in improved patient outcomes and quality of care.[19] However, from a personal perspective, I would consider that there have been benefits to the individual patients that have been presented in supervision and that the learning gained has had a flow-on effect to other patients. In addition, I have gained a greater awareness of my own motivations, influences, and vulnerabilities, assisting me with my personal, professional, and managerial development. Supervision has also contributed to my supervision skills with registrars and medical students. A cohesive supportive supervision group has become a vital component of a professional support system that also includes ongoing contact with mentors, a peer supervision group, contact with trainees (both formal and informal), and attendance at workshops and conferences, be they psychiatric or managerial in focus.

## NOTES

1. Philip Boyce and Margaret Tobin, "Defining the Role of the Consultant Psychiatrist in a Public Mental Health Service," *Australian and New Zealand Journal of Psychiatry* 32, no. 5 (October 1998): 603–11.

2. Jenny Simpson and Richard Smith, "Why Healthcare Systems Need Medical Managers: Doctor Managers Have Distinct Advantages," *British Medical Journal* 314 (June 1997): 1636–37.

3. Australian Health Ministers, *National Mental Health Policy* (Canberra: Australian Government Publishing Service, 1992).

4. Margaret Tobin and Julie Edwards, "Are Psychiatrists Equipped for Management Roles in Mental Health Services?," *Australian and New Zealand Journal of Psychiatry* 36, no. 1 (February 2002): 4–8.

5. Michael A. Silver and Luis R. Marcos, "The Making of the Psychiatrist-Executive," *American Journal of Psychiatry* 146, no. 1 (January 1989): 29–34.

6. Glenn Roberts, Brenda Moore, and Colin Coles, "Mentoring for Newly Appointed Consultant Psychiatrists," *Psychiatric Bulletin* 26, no. 3 (March 2002): 106–9.

7. Donna M. Rose and Philip M. Boyce, "Clinical Supervision and Its Effects on the Quality of Practice of Qualified Practitioners," *Australasian Psychiatry* 7, no. 1 (February 1999): 11–13.

8. Tobin and Edwards, "Are Psychiatrists Equipped for Management Roles in Mental Health Services?," 6.

9. Jenny Simpson and Kenneth Calman, "Making and Preparing Leaders," *Medical Education* 34, no. 3 (March 2000): 211–15.

10. Nigel Edwards, Martin Marshall, Alastair McLellan, and Kamran Abbasi, "Doctors and Managers: A Problem without a Solution? No, a Constructive Dialogue Is Emerging," *British Medical Journal* 326 (March 2003): 609–10.

11. James Reason, "Human Error: Models and Management," *British Medical Journal* 320 (March 2000): 768–70.

12. Lucian L. Leape, "Error in Medicine," *Journal of the American Medical Association* 272, no. 23 (December 1994): 1851–57.

13. Reason, "Human Error," 769.

14. Reason, "Human Error," 770.

15. John Briere, *Therapy for Adults Molested as Children: Beyond Survival* (New York: Springer, 1996), 152–68.

16. Maureen Sayres Van Niel, "Pregnancy: The Obvious and Evocative Real Event in a Therapist's Life," in *Beyond Transference When the Therapist's Real Life Intrudes*, ed. Judith H. Gold and John C. Nemiah (Washington, D.C.: American Psychiatric Press, 1993), 125–40.

17. Nollaig Whyte, "The Analyst's Pregnancy: A Non-Negotiable Fact," *Psychoanalytic Psychotherapy* 18, no. 1 (March 2004): 27–43.

18. Sharon Hopkins, "Pregnancy: An Unthinkable Reality," *Psychoanalytic Psychotherapy* 18, no. 1 (March 2004): 44–66.

19. Rose and Boyce, "Clinical Supervision and Its Effects on the Quality of Practice of Qualified Practitioners," 13.

# 8

# A Hospital-Based Clinician's Experiences of Psychotherapy Supervision

*Mee Ling Khoo*

## EARLY EXPERIENCES

I have worked in mental health for the past twenty-four years, the first five as a psychiatric resident and subsequently as a staff psychiatrist. As a psychiatrist, I have worked continuously, both in private practice and as a part-time staff psychiatrist, with an integrated mental health service based in an inner-city area of a capital city in Australia. For the past sixteen years, I have seen and treated a wide range of patients. At one end of the spectrum are those with chronic psychotic illnesses who live itinerant lives and are on disability support pensions. At the other end are individuals who have been highly successful and functional in their working lives but whose personal lives have been chaotic and dysfunctional. The latter are those referred to by many as the "worried well," a term I would dispute.

I was initially drawn to the prospect of becoming a psychiatrist when, as a first-year medical officer (intern), I admitted a woman in her fifties with her sixth episode of hysterical aphonia. On this occasion, she had presented in a somewhat dramatic fashion from the church where she was to be married for the second time, being unable to say "I do." Taking a personal history from this lady, when she began to speak after thirty-six hours, made me realize why my staff consultant psychiatrist insisted on being presented with detailed personal histories. She would unfailingly ask after each case was presented, "Why has this person presented at this point in time?"

Previously, I had found this insistence frustrating, as it had often meant staying at work late to obtain this information in time for her ward round the next morning. Over the years, I came to realize that, in fact, she had given me a "gift" that has continued to challenge, frustrate, and inspire me in my working life ever since. This psychiatrist subsequently generously made the time to offer to supervise me with this patient. And, as far as I am aware, this patient has not had subsequent presentations for treatment over the past twenty-four years. In therapy, her significant guilt about her previous husband, who had died after a long and complicated illness, emerged. They had had an ambivalent dysfunctional relationship, and she felt intensely guilty about remarriage. Her episodes of aphonia became understandable in the light of her guilt and ambivalence.

The value of this approach to patients has been immeasurable for me, as it taught me that, regardless of diagnosis, every patient is different. Every patient presents a new challenge in terms of my ability to help each person understand him- or herself. It was this experience, as well as the encouragement of other consultants when I did subsequent terms in psychiatry, that helped me decide on my career. However, since then, the outcomes of my attempts to develop expertise in psychodynamics and the psychotherapies, both as resident and as practicing psychiatrist, have been mixed. Nevertheless, I feel that I have learned something from all these experiences, whether they have been positive or negative.

I obtained some competency in cognitive behavior therapy by being supervised by such a therapist for twelve months and continue to update my skills in this area by attending workshops on a regular basis. I find these techniques to be an extremely useful adjunct in helping my patients understand their cognitions and in challenging their thoughts and behaviors. Nevertheless, over the years, I have come to see that, while these techniques provide symptomatic relief, unless we understand the underlying reason for the person's anxiety disorder or need to cross-dress, for example, the symptoms often recur.

My experience of patients, particularly those seen privately, is that the majority try to approach the etiology of their illness by seeking a psychological basis for their symptoms rather than taking prescribed medications. However, they appear to have no issues with taking alternative medications obtained from the health food shop or naturopath.

While there is no doubt that at times there is a purely biological basis for some disorders, even in these situations, to me, an understanding of psychodynamics is necessary to assist our patients. For example, by understanding the likely nature of the therapeutic alliance with patients with a psychotic illness, we are in a better position to assist them in making sense of their illness and decisions regarding their management.[1, 2, 3] Likewise, in managing compliance issues with medication, an understanding of a patient's personality traits or fears of contracting a similar illness to those in their family of origin assists in helping them understand their fears about taking medication.

My psychiatry residency training emphasized the need for a biopsychosocial approach to managing patients. However, in reality, the treatment was, in the main, based on a medical model that was largely biological. In my opinion, this is still how psychiatry is taught in Australia and many other countries and how the majority of psychiatrists treat their patients. On the other hand, as a trainee, I also learned the value of taking a balanced biopsychosocial approach to patients from the experience of being supervised clinically myself. For example, a rigid psychodynamic approach, such as a stance that all patients with bipolar affective disorder, hypomanic phase, were in fact experiencing a "manic defense," was certainly, in my experience, countertherapeutic. Here, ceasing the mood stabilizers and antipsychotic medication while attempting to implement such instructions from one of my clinical psychiatrists in one memorable instance led to chaos on the ward and revolts by nursing staff.

At the time that I trained as a resident, there was little formal training in psychotherapy. My experience of psychodynamics as modeled by my clinical teachers was mainly theoretically based. The lecture programs likewise taught about Freud, Klein, Kohut, Bowlby, Winnicott, and others in a theoretical format. While this was useful certainly in understanding patients, what I had always felt was lacking was learning adequate strategies to manage patients, in particular those with personality disorders.

Textbooks, while extremely informative in terms of helping to theoretically understand patients, in general did not solve treatment dilemmas. The exceptions, for me, were authors such as Gabbard,[4] Sederer,[5] and Malan,[6] whose texts I found—and still find—useful.

As a consequence, I had always felt that I had been inadequately trained in psychodynamic psychotherapy and considered that I would benefit from learning additional skills, particularly in the area of strategies and how to manage patients. This was a feeling that was likewise held by a number of my colleagues and, especially, by two of my friends.

What training was available was, in our opinion, similarly theoretically based and excessively rigid and did not meet our needs. Attending conferences and workshops taught me more about a theoretical understanding but not what to do or say to my patients.

## MY CURRENT PSYCHOTHERAPY SUPERVISOR

Seven years ago, I attended a lecture presented by a new colleague from overseas, an internationally recognized and well-regarded psychotherapist, that was delivered at the invitation of the local branch of the College of Psychiatrists. The content of the lecture stressed, with many examples, the importance of psychotherapeutic skills in everyday clinical practice for psychiatrists. For a number of years, I had been looking for a psychotherapy supervisor and, as a consequence, was sufficiently inspired to find out more about her. Following this, I performed a Medline search of her publications and found them to be practical and clinically applicable to the work I did as a psychiatrist. Several weeks later, when I met her at a lunch organized by a colleague, I felt comfortable with her and, in particular, felt that we shared a common approach to our patients. At the conclusion of lunch, I discussed the possibility of having supervision with her on a regular basis with a group of friends, to which she expressed interest.

At this point, I approached the two friends who had a similar approach to clinical work as myself. While aware of the need to improve our psychotherapeutic skills, we had not, over the years, been able to find a supervisor whom we felt had a similar approach to our clinical work or the level of clinical expertise we sought. We had all known each other for many years and, for a number of years, had provided informal support and "second opinions" for each other.

As a consequence, for seven years we have met every other week for an hour whenever possible. During these sessions, we take turns in presenting material for discussion. The content involves individual cases, family dynamics and issues, and, sometimes, ethical issues as determined by the person presenting. It is also understood that if a member of the group had urgent issues to discuss, this would take priority. At such times, we also have arranged extra, unscheduled supervision sessions.

Of the many skills that we learned over the years, those to do with managing borderline personality disorders have been of most significant benefit to our clinical practice. We came to understand better the psychodynamic challenges of managing one's countertransference and the primitive defenses used by patients, such as projective identification, progressively more over the years. A better understanding of the rapidly changing labile affects and lack of boundaries of this damaged group of people, together with learning strategies to teach our patients to better cope with their fluctuating affects and lack of boundaries, was a continual focus over the years.

Emphasized over and over again was the need to provide containment in the form of clear limits and boundaries in our work with this group of patients. Simultaneously, the need to maximize functioning by assisting these persons to, over time, learn to develop better coping strategies and to validate their gains themselves was also a focus of many of our sessions.

**Case example:** An illustrative case is that of a thirty-year-old woman, not previously treated by myself, admitted after an overdose. (Some details of this case have been altered for confidentiality.) I was contacted by telephone by my resident informing me of her admission. She had an established diagnosis of borderline personality disorder and had had multiple admissions over the past twelve years within the context of significant deliberate self-harm. She had had no admissions for the past twelve months. There appeared to be significant stressors prior to this admission to hospital, including the absence of the case manager who had been seeing this patient weekly for the previous twelve months. The case manager was on a month's annual leave at the time of the overdose. Another significant stressor was the patient's ambivalence, for the preceding weeks prior to her admission, about her decision not to accept an invitation from her father to spend the Christmas period with him and her daughter and grandchild. She had a history of being sexually abused for many years as a child and adolescent by her father.

On the telephone, I discussed with my resident a management plan. I recommended that the patient and nursing staff be actively involved in developing the following guidelines. The admission would be short and focused over a three-day period. It would seek to exclude an Axis I diagnosis according to the *Diagnostic and Statistical Manual of Mental Disorders* (4th ed., text revision), such as a major affective disorder or a psychotic illness. During this time, the patient would work actively with inpatient staff at developing coping strategies to better manage her life when discharged. The patient was to be reviewed on day 3 and be discharged at that point to outpatient care.

On day 3, I was informed by the ward staff that the patient had behaved appropriately and related well to staff and copatients with no evidence of an Axis I diagnosis. However, the prior evening she had been found by nursing staff to have self-inflicted superficial lacerations to her upper body. She was sitting in a fetal position on a chair, rocking, with no eye contact, and repeatedly whispering, "It is not safe for me to leave hospital." Her mood was dysphoric.

My response to the patient's presentation was to understand my countertransference in terms of the projective identification that the patient was displaying. I was aware that I felt frightened and apprehensive and told myself that I was experiencing the patient's feelings which she was projecting onto me, and that she was treating me as if I were the owner of those feelings. Reminding myself of the tendency for these patients to have rapidly changing affects and their lack of boundaries, I proceeded to explore with the patient why she had had no admissions for the previous twelve months. The patient was able to recognize the benefit of the added support and coping strategies that she had acquired from her interactions with her case manager. With encouragement, she was also able to validate the gains that she had made in the past twelve months. These consisted of the absence of deliberate self-harm for twelve months, together with her ability to remain in a supportive relationship with a boyfriend during this period of time. She had also commenced a course that she had attended regularly and was enjoying.

We proceeded to explore the circumstances leading to her overdose and discussed how appropriate her decision to not spend Christmas with her dysfunctional family was. She was able to explore her feelings of abandonment by her case manager during the holiday period while knowing that she would be returning in two weeks. During the interview, her mood became reactive and euthymic. She requested a trial of leave for three days, following which she would be discharged from hospital. We discussed at length about how she would cope over the weekend leave period, including contact from the acute care team. Three days later, I was informed by staff that while the leave had been successful, she had returned to the ward with a black eye that she attributed to a neighbor. She informed staff that she was too frightened to return to her unit as a consequence. Nursing staff also noted that the patient had again deliberately self-harmed in the form of superficial lacerations overnight.

I saw the patient with her case manager, who had returned from leave. She presented as she had three days earlier, sitting in a fetal position, rocking in her chair, saying, "not safe to leave hospital." Again, understanding my countertransference reaction and her labile affect was important. As in the previous occasion, I was aware of my countertransference feelings of fear and a sense of loss of control. Later, discussion with the patient's case manager revealed that she had had the same feelings. We were able to look with the patient at the events of the previous three days and help her recognize that she had in fact coped reasonably well. She was again able to validate her gains and then was able to admit that her black eye had been self-inflicted in an attempt to extend her inpatient stay. She stated that she was scared to be discharged. At this point, she became actively involved in discharge planning, including discussing coping strategies if thoughts of deliberate self-harm returned. Follow-up appointments as an outpatient on a weekly basis with her psychologist case manager, as well as six weekly outpatient sessions with her psychiatrist, were arranged. This psychiatrist was aware of the patient's admission and supportive of her management plan.

An hour later, the case manager returned to inform me that the patient was stating that she had a rope at home with which she intended to hang herself if she was discharged. Additionally, she had informed the case manager that when she was found dead, her father and mother would sue both the hospital and me. We discussed how we would continue to assist the patient in the discharge that had been agreed on that day. We discussed the fact that her inpatient stay had not revealed the presence of an Axis I disorder and that prolonging her inpatient stay would lead most likely to further regression and acts of deliberate self-harm. We agreed that I would not see the patient again that day, as her management plan had not changed, and that the case manager would return to speak to the patient and again discuss the following issues.

She would discuss with the patient her fears of being discharged, again go over the coping strategies that had been discussed, and emphasize why she was to be discharged that day, as it was the opinion of the treating team that she would not benefit from a further period of inpatient admission. A management plan was documented in the chart in the likelihood that she would again self-harm, recommending that further acts of deliberate self-harm be medically managed and that the patient not be admitted to the inpatient psychiatric unit. The department of emergency medicine and the acute care team were contacted and informed of the patient's possible presentation and recommended treatment plan.

When the patient was visited that evening by the acute care team as part of the previously arranged coping strategy plan to assist the patient's transition to outpatient care, she was bleeding copiously from a self-induced laceration. She also informed them that she had swallowed a substantial quantity of caustic soda. As a consequence, the patient was admitted to the intensive care unit for a week and subsequently transferred to a surgical ward. She was discharged directly from the surgery ward at my request to outpatient follow-up. To date, the patient has not self-harmed or had hospital admissions for eighteen months.

I found it most useful to have the opportunity to discuss this case with my supervision group. It allowed me the opportunity to explore my countertransference reaction, particularly to her last—and most serious—attempt at deliberate self-harm. We looked critically at my management plan and, especially, whether I should have discharged her on day 3 rather than allowing her a further period of leave. It was also useful to be able to review the principles of managing persons with borderline personality disorder in terms of understanding not only the psychodynamics involved but also the importance of containment and maximizing functioning. This consisted of being consistent and setting clear limits and getting the patient to self-validate, examine her feelings, and accept responsibility for her management plan. Last but not least was also being able to contain my countertransference.

## THE BENEFITS OF SUPERVISION

Overall, attending this group for the past seven years has enhanced my practical psychotherapeutic skills significantly. I believe that I have a better therapeutic alliance with my patients. I am better able to understand my reactions and am more able to help my patients understand themselves. This has, I feel, then allowed them to make more informed decisions about their lives and to validate and internalize these experiences. The group continues to provide a forum for discussion of challenging cases, ethical issues, and clinical team dynamics.

We have been able to support each other when our supervisor was unavailable, and if particular problems or issues arose at these times, we would discuss them with each other. In addition, the notes that I had taken during our sessions that describe treatment strategies and methods of exploring with the patient what was actually going on have been beneficial.

I consider that supervision such as we have been obtaining for the past seven years has been—and continues to be—of significant benefit for us. In clinical case management oversights and team meetings, we are expected to be the "experts," whereas in this situation I feel that I have learned considerably and added to my clinical skills and acumen. It is sometimes difficult—particularly with patients whom one has been seeing for a number of years and who are, for example, "well cachected" within oneself—to ensure that one's responses in therapy are therapeutic. It is important then for another therapist to "look in" and review together the progress and content of the treatment process. Personally, I am more aware of my obsessionality and tendency to maternal transferences. Supervision has led me to a better understanding of how my obsessionality "drives" me to go to work sometimes when I am sick and that, in some of these situations, my clinical judgment potentially could have been impaired.

The process of being supervised has evolved for us over the past seven years. Our supervisor has moved increasingly from a didactic teaching approach to asking us what we would do and what we thought. Our expectation now is that we will be asked what our observations and strategies are. Increasingly, as I am reviewing the case that I am intending to present, I find that I understand what is occurring in the therapeutic interaction with the patient and on which strategies to focus. In other words, we have been slowly, over time, turned into "supervisors," both of each other and, most important, of ourselves. This has also helped significantly in my own supervision with the residents and mental health professionals with whom I work.

Many of my colleagues understandably feel challenged by having their therapeutic skills exposed by discussion in peer review groups. One might assume that having these skills exposed to a supervisor who has even more skills that oneself would further increase the sense of being shamed. This has in fact not been the case for the group. I feel that there have been two relevant issues here. The first has been that the members of the group (that is, the supervisees) have had long, supportive, and trusting friendships. Just as important, the supervisor's style and approach has been of great significance. We are able to present cases feeling "safe" and not "shamed" even where the supervisor clearly considers that we could have managed the case very differently. She is able to challenge and, at times, be quite confronting without making us feel embarrassed or infantilized. In fact, for myself—and I have no doubt for the three of us—it is a safe place where we can go to find solutions when we feel frustrated and "stuck." Also of significance was the fact that we meet in her home. For me, it has meant a trust in us, which has helped, I feel, in allowing us to reveal our fears and vulnerabilities.

Over the years, supervision, while at times challenging, has been an enjoyable experience where we have learned a great deal. We have also sensed that our supervisor has been less "rigid" in terms of her approach to us and feel that, in fact, she has warmed to us. We have no problem acknowledging that she is our supervisor in our own clinical settings with other staff. As a result of my suggestions to the director of the mental health service where I am employed, our supervisor now also teaches and supervises the residents and allied health professionals in our service.

Occasionally, I will invite the allied health case manager of the patient I am presenting to also be present and contribute to the case I am presenting. This is to allow a more rounded presentation and for them to also learn from the experience. I feel that the envy of other case managers when this occurs is a reflection of how beneficial they have found supervision with our supervisor. Encountering her in social settings for us has been a pleasure, and we have very much enjoyed her company, humor, and humanity.

## NOTES

1. Edward S. Bordin, "The Generalizability of the Psychoanalytic Concept of the Working Alliance," *Psychotherapy: Theory, Research and Practice* 16 (1979): 252–60.
2. Adam O. Horvath, "Relation between Working Alliance and Outcome in Psychotherapy: A Meta-Analysis," *Journal of Counseling Psychology* 38 (1991): 139–49.
3. Arlene F. Frank and John G. Gunderson, "The Role of the Therapeutic Alliance in the Treatment of Schizophrenia," *Archives of General Psychiatry* 47 (1990): 228–36.
4. Glen O. Gabbard, *Psychodynamic Psychiatry in Clinical Practice* (Washington, D.C.: American Psychiatric Publishing, 2005).
5. Lloyd Sederer, *Inpatient Psychiatry: Diagnosis and Treatment* (Baltimore: Williams and Wilkins, 1991).
6. David Malan, *Individual Psychotherapy and the Science of Psychodynamics* (London: Butterworths, 1979).

# 9

# Supervision in Private Practice

*Judy Somerville*

Over the past decade, I have been working in full-time, private psychiatric practice with two colleagues, both of whom also work full time in private practice. The practice is based in the city of Brisbane, Australia, and we have a wide referral basis. We all work quite independently, although we do share an after-hours service. I also do a small amount of resident and student teaching.

During the first few years of practice, I began to identify a number of factors that made this type of work quite different from the experiences I had had in my residency training. In the first section of this chapter, I outline the factors that were evident in my particular practice, with reference to both the type of patient I am most likely to be referred and the type of illnesses they are likely to be suffering from. In the second section of the chapter, I look at how supervision has been useful both in managing these factors and in making my work more rewarding as well as, it is hoped, enhancing patient care.

In the final part of the chapter, I address some factors that are particular to our group supervision and look at some of the changes that have occurred throughout several years of regular supervision.

## FACTORS IDENTIFIED IN PRIVATE PRACTICE

The majority of my training as a resident had, as is usual, taken place in major-city teaching hospitals. We worked on six-month rotations and spent time in a number of different hospitals. My rotations had included time in a war veterans' hospital as well as six months in a prison hospital. My final year, however, at a private psychiatric clinic gave me some early insights into the different types of factors that would be involved in private practice.

The principal factors that presented themselves related to a number of issues. First, the type of patient referred was often quite different from those seen in the hospital system. Second, the type of illness was of a different variety. The overall level of responsibility for the patient enhanced a sense of isolation. This was linked with the commitment to duration of treatment. I now look at each of these factors more specifically.

## Type of Patient

It is hard to identify all the reasons that result in your practice having certain demographics—perhaps it is related to your referral basis, your particular areas of interest, and your gender. My practice now consists of mostly female patients (95 percent) with the majority aged between eighteen and fifty years. The vast majority of my patients will not require a hospital admission at any time for their psychiatric disorder. Those factors alone indicate that I had not had a lot of experience treating people with similar problems in my training years.

Over the years, I have developed a close liaison with a number of general practitioner groups that now form the basis of my referrals. This has many advantages but, at times, increases the "small-town" effect of being referred patients who are known to each other. As a result, confidentiality and privacy issues become paramount within the practice.

## Type of Illness

As you would expect, the previously mentioned demographics determine that a greater number of particular illnesses are seen. Depressive illness (across a broad spectrum) is common and includes acute and chronic, severe and mild, postnatal, and depressive episodes occurring within another illness. Eating disorders (again across a wide spectrum) and anxiety disorders are also seen frequently, as are various manifestations of posttraumatic stress disorder. Personality disorders are well represented with various levels of disability. There are also a number of patients with no diagnosed "illness" per se but who have a number of struggles and difficulties to contend with, including grief and relationship issues.

Once again it becomes apparent that the outpatient management of these illnesses and conditions is not something in which, as a trainee, I had had the opportunity to develop a reasonable amount of experience. I believe, however, that one of the joys of private practice is having the time to develop an understanding of a patient as an individual as well as managing his or her "illness."

## Level of Responsibility

The transition from resident to consultant psychiatrist brings with it an increased level of responsibility, and this factor is of enormous importance in private practice. With it comes the need to outline a short- and long-term management plan as well as establishing liaison with the patient's general practitioner. The level of involvement with the general practitioner is often determined by the working style of that practitioner. In my practice, I encourage my patients to have regular contact with a doctor whom they can trust. A significant number of patients do not have a regular general practitioner, and this may lead to an increase in the level of responsibility felt by the psychiatrist. It is also important to establish other key services, including community services and hospital services, to ensure good quality of care and sharing of responsibility.

## Duration of Treatment

One of the biggest shocks in the establishment of private practice is the realization that, unlike being a trainee, you no longer move on after six months. You, therefore, need to be thinking about management in a different way, with consideration of short-, medium-, and long-term treatment plans and goals. Despite the initial shock that this may bring in the early stages of practice, the benefits of this soon significantly outweigh the negatives. In so many areas of psychiatry, the combination of personal development and time, along with treatment, brings about significant positive changes for the patient. Seeing a patient develop from a late adolescent to a confident adult can be extremely rewarding and a reminder that persistence and patience are very valuable in our field of work.

## Isolation

A combination of the previously mentioned factors may easily result in a sense of isolation. As a trainee, there is often a lot of peer support that occurs "over coffee." In addition, you usually have the luxury of being part of a treatment team with allied supports and services. As mentioned earlier, with the issue of responsibility it is important to develop some strong liaisons with general practitioners and community and hospital services. In our practice, we also share after-hours service provision, and this can significantly reduce the sense of isolation.

## HOW DOES SUPERVISION HELP?

The previously mentioned factors became more evident as my time in private practice continued. Immediately after obtaining certification as a psychiatrist, I had continued to have some involvement with the hospitals. However, the hours in private practice continued to grow. I have always been involved in a peer-review group. However, when two colleagues suggested regular supervision with an experienced supervisor, I leapt at the opportunity. It seemed to be an ideal way to deal with some of the factors described earlier.

### Type of Patient and Duration of Treatment

One of the reasons that I feel our supervision sessions have been so helpful is the fact that our supervisor has such extensive clinical experience. As previously described, my practice has some particular demographics, and our supervisor's experience was very well suited to the type of patient whom I was likely to be treating. I expand on this issue in the next section of the chapter.

In our early sessions, I became increasingly aware of paying attention to detail. I had not necessarily given a lot of thought to the mode of referral; however, in an early presentation, it became apparent that this was quite significant. A patient was referred on a semiurgent basis by a general practitioner with whom I had had a lot of contact. At the time, I was unaware that a good friend of the newly referred person was a patient of mine and that a referral to me had been specifically requested. This became more significant as time progressed, and the two had some conflict. It was extremely useful to discuss the resultant confidentiality and privacy issues in supervision. Patient expectation prior to an appointment, the possibility of idealization, and subsequent denigration were other areas of discussion.

There are many other aspects of mode of referral that can be significant when examined in more detail, and in all our presentations this was discussed. Another patient had attended only because her mother had insisted. On presenting the case, it became apparent that this was a significant factor that had made her hostile about attending. Once this was addressed, she became much more open and trusting. She expressed that she really wanted help but resented her mother's intrusions. She was then able to work on a number of areas in her relationship with her mother and with dependency.

In our earliest presentations, it was evident that we all tended to present the cases that caused us the greatest difficulty. Initially, this meant mainly the angry patients, the hostile patients, the recurrently self-harming patients, and the denigrating patients. It was reassuring to know that we all experienced a similar sense of despair at times in managing these complex and often very distressed patients. Once again, however, the depth of our supervisor's clinical experience enabled us to identify the significant issues and manage the cases more successfully. One of the major issues addressed in these earlier presentations was the setting of reasonable limits and persisting with these. Also involved in this was the discussion of feelings of countertransference that we reassuringly discovered were common to all of us. These feelings were often exacerbated by a sense of hopelessness in our treatment options.

Recurrent presentation of these issues led to a greater sense of direction in treatment. It also meant that with new patients, problem areas could be established early in treatment rather than later and that appropriate management strategies could be instigated in the initial stages. All of this resulted ultimately in better patient care.

As our experience developed, different types of patients became more frequently presented. By this stage, I had been in private practice for several years and had a number of patients whom I had seen for most of that time. With many of these patients, although there did not seem to be any particularly acute issues, it was also difficult to see any significant changes. In most, the history was of long-term depression, fluctuating in severity, frequently with chronic low-grade suicidal ideation and a general sense of hopelessness.

Presenting a number of these cases in supervision, however, offered a number of benefits. First, it required reviewing the case in its entirety. This, in itself, was often revealing, and areas of progress were much more apparent. On a couple of occasions, a forgotten area was recalled. One patient had suffered a significant loss with the death, at an early age, of a sibling. Over years of treatment, this issue had not really been thoroughly explored. Our supervisor's suggestion to address this event further proved to be extremely useful. The patient was able to express a number of grief and guilt feelings she had not previously verbalized.

Discussing a number of long-term patients also allowed for a more objective approach and review. It offered an opportunity to address feelings of helplessness and pessimism. On one occasion, it became apparent that the patient needed her illness as part of her identity. Realizing this allowed me to change my expectations and treatment focus. In general, presenting patients with a long-standing history of symptoms clarified the difficulties involved for each patient in their attempt to change their characteristic thoughts and behaviors. For many, there was a huge level of anxiety about making any change for fear of the consequences. One patient, for example, was able to describe her fear that her marriage would not survive as a result.

Importantly, however, reviewing some long-term patients revealed possible new directions to pursue and reinforced the need for persistence and patience.

## Type of Illness

As mentioned earlier, the types of illnesses I was likely to encounter were commonly encountered in private practice. During the preceding years of training, however, interaction with such patients often occurred in a very different context, usually an inpatient setting when symptoms were acute and severe. Once a crisis had been resolved, patients were often discharged for follow-up elsewhere. Even if there was involvement in the follow-up period, it was time limited. Additionally, while in training, most required a significantly lengthy treatment period.

Once again, attending regular supervision enriched this area of providing long-term psychiatric treatment for patients with a wide variety of diagnoses. It was particularly useful that our supervisor had extensive clinical knowledge and expertise in these areas. The emphasis on paying attention to detail and looking both broadly and laterally at the history often led to different insights and perspectives. Occasionally, presentations dealt with diagnostic dilemmas often revolving around the extent of biological illness versus personality issues and subsequent consequences for treatment. The discussion of one patient clarified her problems were personality based rather than a biological depression. Subsequently, focusing more in treatment sessions on developmental and family issues rather than medication changes resulted in better access to the patient's feelings and low self-worth.

Presenting diagnostic dilemmas was useful for both long-term patients and new presentations. On a number of occasions, patients were presented over time as their psychotherapeutic treatment progressed, and diagnostic issues could be reconsidered.

Mostly, however, the focus during supervision sessions has been not on the diagnosis per se but on looking more deeply at the patient as a whole. For me this has definitely been one of the highlights of having an experienced clinician to whom to present cases. Our supervisor has always highlighted the individual characteristics of each patient presented and drawn together elements from their developmental history, their family of origin, and personality features. Looking at the patient in a broader context has also been encouraged. Our supervisor has steered us to look at all the patient's relationships, not just those in the immediate family. This has been especially valuable when addressing issues associated with low self-worth and self-esteem, as it has enabled me to help patients also look more broadly at themselves as well as their capabilities and resources. In one particular case of chronic depression and family disharmony, the patient gradually used her friendships with two close friends to develop a more accurate assessment of her self-worth.

Looking extensively at a patient's relationships has also often helped patients put their relationships into a different perspective. One of the recurring issues during presentations has been the importance of developing an understanding of the factors involved for those people close to the patient. Encouraging patients to develop a greater level of objectivity about those around them allows for much greater insights and also results in reducing their level of anger and increasing their level of acceptance. One patient made significant gains when she began to understand the factors that had led to her father's alcoholism. She was able to let go of a huge amount of anger and begin to see that his behavior was not specifically about her. This issue of increasing objectivity has been enormously useful on many occasions in my practice. It has often allowed for anger to be replaced by sadness and even empathy and has encouraged many to distance themselves a little and not interpret events and actions so personally.

Another similar recurring theme that has become more evident through attending supervision is the feeling a number of patients have described of somehow not "fitting" with either their family or their friends. Once again, learning to be more objective about those around them has encouraged a number of people to alter their expectations and become more focused on the things in their life that do offer them a sense of belonging. Instead of looking desperately for change, they have a better opportunity to become who they really are in a supported environment.

## Level of Responsibility

As previously mentioned, one of the daunting factors involved in patient care in private practice is the level of responsibility felt for the patient's care and well-being. Once again, supervision provides an opportunity for some of the issues involved to be addressed. First, it frequently puts into perspective an appropriate level of responsibility. The process of sharing concerns for a particular patient is an opportunity to discuss specific areas of worry, especially the issue of chronic suicidal ideation and recurrent self-harm. Our supervisor has highlighted the benefits of having a strong therapeutic alliance with the patient, with the concomitant awareness of higher levels of distress. There is also the practical issue of utilization of other services at times of significant concern that may involve access to community and hospital services as well as involvement of significant family or friends.

Once again, supervision has been extremely useful in dealing with the broader issue of responsibility for a patient through reviewing management issues and confronting transference and countertransference factors that address many of the factors involved in responsibility. One of the major areas has been the development of responsibility by the patient, a process often integral to becoming well.

### Isolation

Over the years of working in a busy private practice, it has become apparent how easily a sense of isolation can develop despite sharing an office suite with two other practitioners. There rarely is time to interact with each other let alone discuss management issues in a general sense. Being a part of a supervision group has definitely helped with this potential feeling of isolation.

Importantly, presenting a case allows for a feeling of shared concern. One of the particular factors of our group has been how similar many of the problems presented have been. This in itself is enormously reassuring. Knowing that the same issues trouble your colleagues decreases that sense of aloneness that can occur in private practice. We have all learned from the experience of the others. It is not only important to seek and gain reassurance regarding your therapeutic skills. It is also vital to feel able to ask for help and acknowledge areas of professional insecurity.

Another important aspect of our supervisory group is the diversity of practice. My colleagues work in different practice settings and, hence, will also present some types of cases that I no longer encounter. This has been enormously valuable as a way of remaining up to date with clinical (and even nonclinical) practice. I feel sure that we have learned as equally from each other's presentations as from our own, and for me this has significantly reduced the isolation of private practice.

## WHAT HAS WORKED FOR US IN SUPERVISION

We have been meeting for group supervision on a regular basis for several years. On many occasions, only two of us (or sometimes even only one of us) are able to meet. We attempt to meet on average once per month for one hour with one case presented each time. We would all agree that the most important factor in our experience of supervision being so useful and rewarding has been the supervisor herself.

From my perspective of working full time in private practice, the supervisor's clinical background provides a wealth of material. One of the most useful aspects of supervision in this setting has been her description of clinical experiences of her own (and their subsequent outcome) with relevance to the case being discussed. Not only does this allow for comparisons with similar scenarios, but it also offers the opportunity to see how a particular intervention was helpful. Perhaps the most useful and practical aspect of this has been the fact that she will suggest quite specifically some things to say to a patient. As a group, we have garnered a number of these very useful suggestions and can now utilize them ourselves at appropriate times.

Another aspect has been her style of supervision. She is open to discussing all aspects of a patient's care, as was alluded to in the earlier part of this chapter, and has made us aware of the need to have a full understanding of the patient, not just the symptoms or diagnosis. She has frequently alerted us to aspects of a patient's personal, developmental, or relationship history that may have a significant impact on their illness or behavior. Dynamic factors and transference issues are also discussed. Other aspects of treatment are also addressed, as necessary, including pharmacological treatments and cognitive-behavioral approaches. The potential use of other support services and interventions are also considered when appropriate.

In addition, aspects of confidentiality and ethics are an integral part of the process. The supervisor has always reinforced the need for maintaining thorough and detailed notes and providing education and feedback to patients. She has addressed the issue of setting appropriate goals and having well-thought-through management plans. Once again, these aspects of her supervision reflect her knowledge and understanding of a clinical workload. All those factors referred to earlier as being the potential hazard areas of private practice are assisted by this comprehensive approach to supervision.

The second—and again enormously important—successful factor in our supervision experience has been the group itself. I have known both other supervisees for many years and have shared various work and social experiences with them. Throughout the years of having supervision together, it has become apparent that we all work in a somewhat similar way—we are all essentially eclectic in our approach and utilize both biological and psychological treatment interventions. We are all very comfortable and trusting with each other, and this leads to not only an open approach to presenting cases but also a greater level of honesty. I feel these things are vital for truly useful supervision to occur. The capacity to confront potential mistakes or difficulties, while initially intimidating, is actually what allows for real development in practice to proceed. As a group, I feel we have become even more comfortable with each other (as well as with our supervisor) over time.

Another aspect of our particular group is the level of flexibility. As mentioned, on many occasions we are not all able to attend. As a result, the issue of who presents a case is often determined only at the last minute. On some occasions, one of the group may feel a greater need to present a case, and the group happily accommodates these factors. As previously mentioned, we all feel that we have learned from every case or situation presented, not just our own. Lastly, as a group, including our supervisor, we all share one invaluable asset—a sense of humor.

Over the period of time that we have been having supervision, there have been some gradual changes. As already discussed, we have all become more comfortable about presenting cases and as a result are more relaxed and open. We are now more able to identify a problem area and focus on that early in the presentation. We frequently have the opportunity to update the group on a case that has previously been presented, giving us all the opportunity to see progress and outcomes. The type of patient likely to be presented is now more diverse, with often a particular theme or issue raised for discussion. We are also more likely to discuss issues as a group rather than to rely on our supervisor for sole comments. After each session, however, almost invariably we will all comment on the value of attending.

I believe that I have highlighted that attending supervision has benefits not only for the practitioner but also for overall patient care. This occurs not only directly with respect to specific patients presented but also indirectly in terms of dealing with recurring themes and areas of difficulty. For me, the process of attending supervision has meant that I feel I have a support group behind me rather than feeling the isolating effects of a busy private practice. When seeing a patient, I can often reflect on similar issues previously presented and develop a sense of understanding and direction from that. It has helped me deal with ethical and responsibility issues and allowed me to look in a much broader and inclusive way at management of patients. It has helped me identify the slow process of change and become generally more persistent as well as patient. I feel that attending supervision will continue to be a part of my clinical practice for the rest of my working life, and I would strongly recommend it to any other practitioner working in private practice.

# Index

# About the Editor and Contributors

**Judith H. Gold, CM, MD, FRCPC, FRANZCP,** currently practices psychiatry privately in Brisbane, Australia, where she is also a psychodynamic psychotherapy supervisor for psychiatrists and other mental health professionals and is involved in psychotherapy teaching with psychiatric trainees. As a visiting professor from 1998 to 1999, she established a chair in psychotherapy at the University of Queensland. Previously, she was in private psychotherapy practice in Halifax, Nova Scotia, Canada, having been an associate professor of psychiatry at Dalhousie University. She is a past president of the Canadian Psychiatric Association and the American College of Psychiatrists. She received the Order of Canada (CM) for her work promoting the education and health of women and minorities. She was editor of the Clinical Practice series of the American Psychiatric Press Inc. from 1987 to 2002.

**Norman A. Clemens, MD,** is clinical professor of psychiatry at the Case Western Reserve University School of Medicine, Cleveland, Ohio. He is president and a training and supervising analyst in the Cleveland Psychoanalytic Center and is in the private practice of psychiatry and psychoanalysis. He is editor of the psychotherapy columns of the *Journal of Psychiatric Practice* and coeditor of psychotherapy columns of *Psychiatric Services*. He chaired the Commission on Psychotherapy by Psychiatrists of the American Psychiatric Association from 1996 to 2000.

**Marcia Kraft Goin, MD, PhD,** is professor of clinical psychiatry, University of Southern California Keck School of Medicine, and director of residency training, Adult Psychiatric Outpatient Department, Los Angeles County/University of Southern California. She is a past president of the American Psychiatric Association and was chair of the Committee on Psychotherapy by Psychiatrists. She is a member of the American Psychoanalytic Association, the American Academy of Psychoanalysis and Psychodynamic Psychotherapy, and the New Center for Psychoanalysis. She is editor of a column on psychotherapy of *Psychiatric Services*.

**Mee Ling Khoo, MBBS, FRANZCP,** is a general adult psychiatrist working in both the public and the private sector in Brisbane, Australia. She enjoys the diversity of working with a multidisciplinary team based in an inner-city mental health service as well as teaching medical students and psychiatric trainees. In her private practice, she treats predominantly women with a variety of mental disorders from all walks of life.

**Robert Michels, MD,** is the Walsh McDermott University Professor of Medicine and Psychiatry, Cornell University, and training and supervising analyst, Columbia University Center for Psychoanalytic Training and Research.

**Jacinta Powell, MBBS, FRANZCP, MHA,** has been a psychiatrist for eleven years. She is currently director of the Inner North Brisbane Mental Health Service, Australia, and previously was director of mental health for the State of Queensland, Australia. She is chair of the Queensland branch of the Royal Australian and New Zealand College of Psychiatrists and has had an active role in the education of psychiatric trainees.

**Gail Erlick Robinson, MD, DPsych, FRCPC,** is a professor of psychiatry and obstetrics/gynecology at the University of Toronto, Ontario, Canada. She is the director of the Women's Mental Health Program at the University Health Network. She has written, designed courses, acted as an expert witness, and lectured extensively on the subject of boundaries in fiduciary relationships.

**Judy Somerville, MBBS, FRANZCP,** is in full-time practice of psychiatry in Brisbane, Australia. She obtained her qualification in psychiatry in 1993, and from 1993 to 1996 she was both a lecturer at the University of Queensland and in half-time psychiatry practice. Currently she remains involved in teaching medical students and psychiatry trainees.

**Francis T. Varghese, MBBS, FRANZCP,** is a psychiatrist in private practice and associate professor at the University of Queensland, Brisbane, Australia. He supervises mainly psychiatric residents in psychotherapy. His current research includes using a psychodynamic supervision model in assisting primary care physicians in the care of the terminally ill.

www.ingramcontent.com/pod-product-compliance
Ingram Content Group UK Ltd.
Pitfield, Milton Keynes, MK11 3LW, UK
UKHW012042150926
475560UK00001B/140

9 780765 703996